COMBAT ADVISOR

COMBAT ADVISOR

HOW AMERICA WON THE WAR AND LOST THE PEACE IN VIETNAM

WITH A WARNING ABOUT IRAQ

JOHN C. LOVING

iUniverse, Inc.
New York Lincoln Shanghai

Combat Advisor
How America Won the War and Lost the Peace in Vietnam

Copyright © 2006 by John C. Loving

iUniverse books may be ordered through booksellers or by contacting:

iUniverse
2021 Pine Lake Road, Suite 100
Lincoln, NE 68512
www.iuniverse.com
1-800-Authors (1-800-288-4677)

ISBN-13: 978-0-595-39107-3 (pbk)
ISBN-13: 978-0-595-83495-2 (ebk)
ISBN-10: 0-595-39107-9 (pbk)
ISBN-10: 0-595-83495-7 (ebk)

Printed in the United States of America

This book is dedicated to my children and grandchildren, so that they will know what their papa did during the Vietnam War.

CONTENTS

ACKNOWLEDGMENTS

This book is based primarily upon my recollection of events that took place between April 1969 and January 1970 while serving in Vietnam as an advisor to Regional Forces in the Army of the Republic of Vietnam.

I owe a debt of gratitude to the people who supported me and assisted me in this writing, which took place over a period of about ten years. My wife, Lennis, gave me much support and provided valuable assistance with editing and organizing the text. My sons David and Matthew; my stepdaughter Lennis Tugman and her husband Kurt, and my stepson Lawson Bennett endured many hours of listening to my numerous war stories, a process that helped to preserve the record in my mind.

Additionally, my friend Tom Skidmore, who is a veteran of World War II, spent much time reading and editing my manuscript, and my former classmate from the University of Richmond, Major General Warren C. Edwards (U.S. Army ret.) provided credible insight into the situation in Iraq as it relates to America's experience in Vietnam.

Lastly, I must thank my old friend and comrade in arms, Command Sergeant Major Mack F. Rice (U.S. Army Ret.), who added his memories to mine, and in particular helped reconstruct the events of the Cambodian Incursion by our Regional Forces units in October 1969.

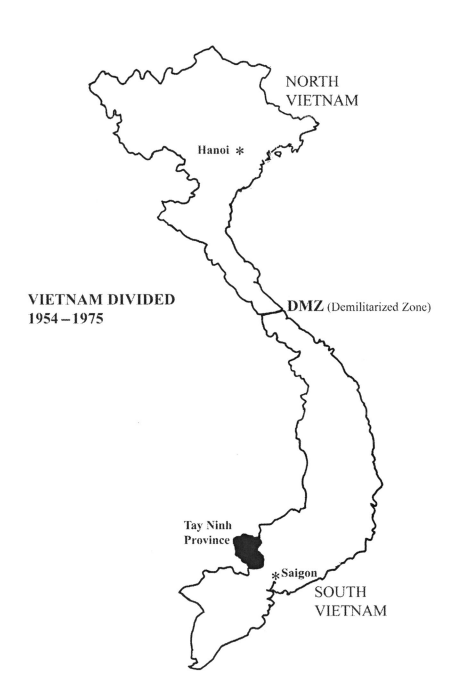

NORTH
VIETNAM

Hanoi ✳

VIETNAM DIVIDED
1954–1975

DMZ (Demilitarized Zone)

Tay Ninh
Province

✳ Saigon

SOUTH
VIETNAM

PROLOGUE

As I begin this account of my experiences as a combat infantry advisor to Vietnamese Regional Forces in the Army of the Republic of Vietnam, I realize that every soldier has a story to tell. This story is very personal but has value for both the hearer and the teller. As our country embarks on an era of seemingly inevitable military conflicts in foreign lands, I am writing with two purposes in mind. My first goal is to describe lessons learned in the Vietnam War that have relevance to these modern-day conflicts.

My second goal is to accomplish a personal inventory of times and events that have profoundly affected my life. It is by no means an exaggeration to say that my tour in Vietnam forever changed the way I view life and living, and in no small part helped shape the man I am today.

In the movie *Patton*, George C. Scott, who plays the role of the great General George Patton, speaks to his unit, the U.S. Third Army, which is assembled in a large auditorium. He tells them that although their impending deployment to the war in Europe will be difficult duty, "when your grandchildren sit on your lap and ask you 'what did you do during the war, grandpa,' you won't have to say 'I shoveled shit in Louisiana.'" The general was not the most diplomatic of speakers, but he did accurately describe the major benefit that comes to a combat soldier, the right to say "I was there."

In this account, I recall experiences that were significant to me, which will certainly include those instances of real combat, but also the things I remember about the land and the people, and a bit about everyday life in the "Nam." I have attempted to relate the events as accurately as possible, and to substantiate them wherever possible with written records. Unfortunately, I do not remember the names of all the people, especially the Vietnamese, and in some instances I have used nicknames or assigned names to help keep them straight or to preserve reputations.

It has been estimated that only one out of five military personnel serving in Vietnam was actually in a combat role. As an army infantry officer, I happened to be one of those combatants. Many officers and enlisted men never saw combat and still performed valuable service. Some actually had fairly comfortable experiences during the war. I met a young infantry lieutenant in Saigon who was working at an office job at MACV (Military Assistance Command Vietnam) headquarters and living in a trailer with his mother, who was a defense department employee. He probably never heard a shot fired the whole time he was there. Despite the infantry insignia on his collar, he confided to me that he did not have to worry about being transferred to any kind of combat job because his mother would not stand for it.

Except for one week of R&R (rest and recuperation), I spent my entire time in a combat role. There were other men who were assigned combat positions but still saw very little action. My tour, on the other hand, was well sprinkled with events that were extraordinary and, at times, even terrifying. A sniper shot at me the third day I was in the field, the Vietcong (VC) tried to blow me up with mines planted in the road to our compound two weeks before I left, and I cannot say how many times I came under attack from either small arms or mortars during the time in between. There is an old saying in the military that "war is made up of days of boredom and drudgery interspersed with moments of terror." That was certainly true in Vietnam.

I tried to do my duty as best I could, because I never wanted to look back and be ashamed of my conduct. In the novel *The Catcher in the Rye*, J. D. Salinger quotes William Stekel as saying, "The mark of the immature man is that he wants to die nobly for a cause, while the mark of the mature man is that he wants to live humbly for one." Despite the fact that our cause in Vietnam was not always clear, I believe that our men fought honorably, and deserve the gratitude of our nation. There seems to be more effort today than at any time in the past thirty years to separate our Vietnam warriors from the war itself, and to give them the credit they are due. They are recognized now as having persevered in the face of considerable hardship and danger, and for doing their duty as American soldiers who fought on behalf of an American people not fully committed to the cause.

During my tour of duty, I did make mistakes, and I do have regrets. Most Americans now look back and think that the Vietnam War was a great waste, and we say it was a tragedy that soldiers have died in such a war. I would say it is also a tragedy to have killed other men in such a war. Nevertheless, for the most part, I fought well. I carried the fight to the enemy, and did him as much damage as possible without unduly endangering my men. If that was wrong, may God forgive me.

From the day I graduated from ROTC at the University of Richmond, it was inevitable that I would go to Vietnam. When I received my new uniforms from the U.S. Army, I took them to my mother to sew on my insignia. Watching her accomplish this task reminded me of sitting beside her as a small child, thinking how marvelous she was at being able to make or mend clothes for herself and our family. As her nimble fingers stitched on the small patches that identified my rank and branch of service, she asked, "What do these little crossed rifles mean?"

"They mean I'm in the infantry," I said proudly.

She shook her head sadly and said, "You are educated, let others do the fighting."

Seeing her concern, all I could say was, "Don't worry, Mom. I'll be OK." After that, my impending departure to the war was almost never mentioned, but we all knew that I would have to go soon. Mom did worry, and she told me when I got back that while I was in Vietnam, she feared that she would "wear God out" praying for me.

As I undertake this writing in early 2006, our country is embroiled in a situation in Iraq that is, in some ways, similar to what we experienced in Vietnam. We were then, and we are now, fighting against an insurgency that is highly motivated, resourceful, fearless, and ruthless. As in Vietnam, we already have made a substantial commitment of men and materials, and yet we seem no better off than when we started. How did we get to this point?

The road to war was laid on September 11, 2001, when we experienced deadly attacks on Washington DC and on the World Trade Center in New York City, by an extremist group identified as al-Qaeda. After a year or so of planning, we undertook a successful counterattack on the enemy in Afghanistan, and then invaded Iraq with patriotic fervor. Now, after our quick and seemingly decisive defeat of the Iraqi army, we find ourselves cast in the role of occupiers—in a land as foreign to our own as exists in the world today.

If there is one lesson that we should have learned in Vietnam, it is that the American military is very good at winning military battles but very poor at conducting successful occupations. Some would say that this is good, that our country has no business occupying other countries and that the national conscience is opposed to it. There is certainly merit in this argument, but the reality is that we are in the unfortunate position that General Colin Powell, former Chairman of The Joint Chiefs of Staff, warned us about before the first war with Iraq: "If we break it, we own it." Now that we have "broken" the country of Iraq, we must either stay long enough to fix it, or we must abandon it to others to pick up the pieces. The others who are likely to step into the void created by our departure include Iran and Syria, joined by a sizable contingent of operatives from al-Qaeda and from Hamas, the radical Palestinian regime.

There is a considerable political debate raging today in our country, and in the world for that matter, about whether we should have gone into Iraq at all, about whether the American people were misled regarding the existence of weapons of mass destruction, and about whether our government had ulterior motives such as the desire for oil reserves. There is nothing being said in this debate that will help extract us from the mess in which we now find ourselves. The only relevant question today is this: How do we get out with honor, and without throwing the people of Iraq to the radical wolves waiting at the door?

I believe that one answer lies in our experience in Vietnam and the lessons we learned there. Yes, the Vietnam War was a quagmire, a national tragedy, and a political nightmare that brought down a president and wasted many American lives. Nevertheless, it holds in its history the answers to our present dilemma. Iraq is not, of course, Vietnam, but the situation we are in today is certainly similar to the one we were in then. The real question is whether we will do any better today at removing ourselves from the desert of Iraq than we did removing ourselves from the quagmire of Vietnam. If we do anything other than just pull out and abandon the country, which is unlikely, the answer will lie in the success of our effort to turn the fighting over to the Iraqi military. If we do prevail in this effort, it will be because we have a strong, well-trained, and well-organized advisory effort imbedded with the military of Iraq.

The spring 2006 issue of *Counterparts*, a newsletter devoted to Vietnam advisors, reprinted an e-mail that was received from a sergeant in the U.S. Army. It read as follows:

Gentlemen
My name is Kelly Mann. I am a Cav. Scout in the 4th Infantry Division, United States Army, currently deployed to Iraq. This is my second tour. I and others have been selected to be advisors to the New Iraqi Army. While doing a search to find information about my mission, I came across your website. We are currently undergoing a train-up, mostly consisting of classroom instruction. Most of the info we have received has been informative. This is a new program that was just started this last year, so most of the info we get is based on trial and error. I was wondering if anybody from your group would be willing to send us info, advice, or personal experiences that can help us out. Though we have received a couple of SF briefs, we are

pretty much going into this blind. My team is very motivated about this assignment as am I. We know it will be tough, demanding and frustrating at times, but we know it will be very rewarding. Any help will be appreciated. Thank you for your time.

Sincerely,
SFC Kelly M. Mann
U.S. Army

If the United States is to be successful in extracting itself from Iraq without turning it over to our mortal enemies, it will be because of men and women like Sergeant Mann. He is right. It will be tough—and it will be near impossible without extended and dangerous effort on his part and those who, like Mann, are selected to be advisors. Iraq has become less a war than an occupation. The longer we remain as occupiers, the more we will incite the hatred of the Iraqi people, and thus the growth of the insurgency. Our only chance for success is to provide trained, professional soldiers to the Iraqi military, soldiers who will show them how to take up the fight as we leave. If the people who undertake this effort understand the lessons learned in Vietnam, they will be more likely to succeed.

Looking beyond Iraq, it is likely that most of our future conflicts will also involve less traditional massive military campaigns and more of these limited military operations that feature occupations and fighting against insurgencies. These military campaigns will require advisory efforts to support friendly forces in the fight against insurgency elements. This is being done successfully in Afghanistan, and could probably have been done in Iraq if our leaders had realized how quickly the organized elements of the Iraqi army would disintegrate.

Hindsight is perfect, of course, but it seems likely that, as Iraqi military elements surrendered to our people, some units could have been retained intact and turned against the resistance. This would have left us looking more like allies and less like occupiers. Now we will have to rebuild and reequip those units, which will require a strong advisory effort on the part of our military.

Although this book is primarily a collection of my experiences, I have made a concerted effort to detail many of the pitfalls that the United States encountered with the advisory effort in Vietnam, and to explore how we dealt with them on a small unit level. Some were handled successfully and others were not, but they all offer lessons about training and operating with military counterparts in foreign lands.

In part, then, this book is offered to Sergeant Mann and his fellow advisors so that they can learn from the experiences of a small group of his predecessors—soldiers who tackled the challenges of advising the military officers and men in another land, on the other side of the world.

CHAPTER 1

DESTINED FOR COMBAT

Every man thinks meanly of himself for not having been a soldier, or not having been at sea.

—James Boswell, *Life of Samuel Johnson* (1791)

I graduated from the University of Richmond in 1967. I had been enrolled in ROTC there during my four years of study, and the day I received my diploma, I also received a commission as a second lieutenant in the U.S. Army. ROTC had been a good experience for me, but I cannot say that I knew a whole lot about the army or about combat when I finished. My military classes had been quite rudimentary, and it seemed that most of the tactics I learned came from military history class, which concentrated quite a bit on the Civil War. As I look back, however, I realize that my training had started much earlier. It actually started when I was a youngster growing up in West Point, a small rural town in eastern Virginia

As a boy, I had always felt destined for some form of combat, and many things were placed into my path to prepare me for it. It started in the fourth grade when my teacher, a retired naval commander, was discussing his experiences during World War II. He seemed to be looking squarely at me when he said, "Some of you boys will most likely end up in a war at some time in your life. Just about every generation has had its war, and yours should be no exception." From that day forward I felt I was bound to fight somewhere, some time, and I began to mentally prepare myself for it.

As I grew older, I began to believe that I would some day assume the role of one summoned to defend his country, what is called a citizen soldier. This was not a sudden realization but a gradual acceptance of what seemed to me to be inevitable, and I came to understand this future role as being obligatory and not optional. My studies in history produced many examples to emulate, and I embraced them not as superheroic characters but as ordinary people caught up and transformed by the extraordinary experience of war. I studied Lucius Cincinnatus, Roman statesman, soldier, and farmer, who lived around 450 BC. After serving some time as a soldier and statesman in Rome, he returned to his farm on the other side of the Tiber River to finish his life as an ordinary citizen, but soon after his retirement to this bucolic life, a large army of barbarians from the east threatened his country. When the Roman Army was surrounded and threatened with annihilation, the Roman Senate voted to offer Cincinnatus the title of emperor for a period of six months if he would return and save the country. A delegation was sent to his farm across the river where he was found plowing his field behind a team of oxen. Naturally he accepted the challenge, returned to Rome where he raised an army and defeated the invaders. After being emperor for only sixteen days he went back before the Senate, gave up his crown of power, and returned to his fields.

Growing up in the historically rich Old Dominion (Virginia), there were also plenty of homegrown examples of famous citizen soldiers to enforce my belief in the necessity and certitude of fulfilling this role. Like Cincinnatus, George Washington left his farm in northern Virginia to lead American forces in defeating the British, served his time as president and then returned to Virginia and the green fields of his plantation. My own ancestor, Private William Hansboro was part of his army; a fact that I felt sure helped seal the fate of the Red Coats at Yorktown. Further evidence of my inevitable sojourn with the military came when I learned of my great-grandfather, Henry Vaughter Loving, who served under Stonewall Jackson during the Civil War. He was a farmer from Louisa County, Virginia, who joined the Confederate Army in 1862 just before the battle of Fredericksburg and was still serving when General Robert E. Lee surrendered at Appomattox in April 1865. He was a small farmer who owned no slaves but answered the call when The State of Virginia asked her sons to defend her sacred soil from the impending invasion from the North. He was a short, thin man with little education, however, I believe him to be a man of grit since he was still with the army at the very end when most of the others had deserted and gone home.

Like my ancestors, I learned to shoot a rifle and a shotgun at an early age, and spent many hours outdoors, learning the ways of the woods, the fields, and the streams. In high school, I enjoyed history and literature. I played trumpet in the band, and since both of my parents were highly musical, I was expected to be a natural. Unfortunately, I proved to be less than spectacular with this instrument. During a particularly difficult practice session, the band instructor threw up his hands in frustration and said, "I don't know how anyone with your parents could be so unmusical." I remarked that I had been wondering the same thing, and suggested that I quit. He readily agreed, and so I sold the trumpet and bought a shotgun.

As a young man, several lessons in leadership and team organization helped prepare me for my eventual role as a unit leader. Playing on the high school football team, for example, taught me the importance of leadership and team-work. Because I weighed only 136 pounds at the time, the experience was also a lesson in toughness and perseverance, and I learned that determination and spirit can overcome size and strength. I also joined the high school rifle team where—unlike the school band—I proved to be a natural: When I arrived at the University of Richmond, I was readily accepted on the varsity rifle team.

At the end of my senior year in high school, I had another experience that taught me the value of leadership when I worked a summer job with my brother, David. Our job was to clear land for the local paper mill, and I was crew chief of a team of five boys. We worked in the woods around West Point, clearing unharvested hardwood trees so that pine seedlings could be replanted.

We swung axes all day in the hot sun, and I learned how to lead a group of young men, to coax them to keep going even when they didn't want to work. Our boss was a wise man named Claiborne Courtney. He was able to sneak up on us without being detected, and in the beginning he would check up on us most days. Some days we would work our way through a grove of trees to find him waiting for us at the end. After a few weeks, he mostly left us alone because he soon learned that I would keep the boys working whether he was there or not. At the end of the second year, he told me that we had cleared more acres of land per dollar expended than any other crew. I really appreciated this compliment, as it came from a man I respected a great deal.

At the end of that summer, I started school at the University of Richmond. Richmond is a University with a strong liberal arts program, and it seemed perfect for one, like myself, who was undecided about careers and majors. An older friend who was in the ROTC program there reminded me of the military draft and said, "If you have to go, you might as well go as an officer." This seemed like good reasoning to me so I enrolled in the course. I found the ROTC classes to be interesting, and I made good grades. My senior year I was selected to serve on battalion headquarters staff and was promoted to major. Of course, when my branch assignment arrived, it read "infantry." Although I never considered a career in the army, I had always presumed that I would someday assume my role as citizen soldier, and by the summer of 1967, that day was fast approaching. I graduated with a bachelors of arts degree in economics.

After working for nine months as a National Bank examiner in the U.S. Treasury Department, I entered the active army in April 1968. Although I already had a commission, the army knew that new ROTC officers were not ready for combat and sent me to Fort Benning, Georgia, to the Infantry Officers Basic Training Course. At Benning, junior officers received some fairly intensive training in tactics and weapons, consisting of both classroom instruction and field exercises. For the most part, my instructors were usually men who had been severely wounded in the war and were no longer fit for combat. Oddly enough, many had been wounded by the very weapon they were teaching.

The artillery instructor had had the left side of his face blown away by a mortar round. His face had been cleverly rebuilt with plastic, and his deformity was not detectable from a distance. The captain who taught us to fire and disassemble the 50-caliber machine gun proudly told us that his withered right arm, which dangled limply from his shirtsleeve, had in fact been hit with a 50-caliber round. There also was the African American sergeant who taught us how to use plastic explosives. He had an almost featureless face, which while black was splotched white where it had obviously been badly burned. These men were sober reminders to young lieutenants that Vietnam was not a B-rated movie but, rather, a place where we needed to be very careful and know what we were doing.

At Fort Benning, I soon discovered that several life-lessons needed to be learned outside of the classroom. I had to quickly learn to deal with other men whose backgrounds were very different from my own—men of many different races, religions, and cultures. They were from all walks of life, some highly educated, others who had come up through the enlisted ranks, and a few who had received battlefield commissions.

My roommate, Grady, was a highly unusual individual who was, at times, amusing and, at other times, frustrating but never boring. He was a young man from Oklahoma who loved to have a good time. Grady was short and stocky, solidly built, and spoke with a strong, Southwestern accent. I suspect that every group has its wild man, and Grady was ours. Soon after we arrived at Fort Benning, Grady discovered that some of the wives sitting around the pool at the Officers Club were not exactly pining away while their husbands did their tours in Vietnam. He spent a lot of his time at night dancing and drinking with these ladies. I remember a particular night when he didn't come in at all, and the next morning at roll call, he still wasn't there.

After roll call, we all climbed into the back of large, open trucks to go to the field, and as I looked back toward our quarters, I saw him come running out with his shirt unbuttoned and his boots untied. Running as fast as he could, he managed to catch up with our truck before we got out of the parking lot, and I pulled him aboard. "Where the hell have you been?" I exclaimed. He looked down as he buttoned his shirt, thinking hard like he wasn't sure.

Finally he said, "Well, I went out dancing and drinking, and…" After a long pause, he added, "Well, there was this woman in town." That was all he could manage to say, and it was enough.

Grady, part Cherokee, said to me one evening at the Officers Club that he thought the stories about Indians and firewater were true. A heavy drinker, he seemed to get totally drunk after only one beer but remained in that same state, no drunker, through the next five or six beers. When he drank and danced, he sweated profusely, and he constantly came back to our room to borrow my shirts because his were soaking wet from dancing in the hot night air. One night after I had gone to sleep, he came in, cut on the light, and asked if he could borrow a shirt. I said sure, rolled over and opened my eyes. To my surprise, there was a rather frumpy looking blond woman sitting on the edge of my bed. Grady introduced her to me, and I said "hello" without sitting up. She quickly kissed me on the cheek, and in a flash, they were both out the door to continue their night of revelry. While trying to get back to sleep, I wondered what her husband was doing at that time 9,000 miles away in Vietnam.

After awhile, Grady and some of the other guys in the troop discovered a whorehouse in town. This became a favorite place for Grady to go when there was no action with the ladies on post. On one of those trips to the whorehouse, Grady and the others took a young man who was a newly ordained chaplain. The next day, Grady tried to collect the $25 he had paid to the madam on the chaplain's behalf, but the chaplain refused to pay. The chaplain admitted to getting pretty drunk that night, but he was sure he had not sinned in the house of ill repute. Grady never forgot that he had not been reimbursed and always said that he figured the chaplain was just too ashamed of himself to confess that he owed the $25. Grady said that he would not take me to the whorehouse because he knew that I was getting married when the training was over, and he didn't want me to give my new wife the clap. I must admit that I wasn't disappointed, but I did wonder why he didn't worry about giving *his* wife the clap.

One Friday night near the end of the course, Grady told me that he had met a girl in town and thought he was in love. He wanted me to meet her, and since we had no training planned for the next morning, I agreed to drive Grady into town to meet his new girlfriend. We left the post about mid-morning the next day, and as I followed his directions, I soon realized that we were entering a rather shabby part of town. After several turns off the beaten path, he had me stop in front of a bar on a dirty street where most of the buildings were dilapidated and many were vacant. The large plate-glass window at the front of the bar was cracked and held together with several pieces of duct tape.

I followed Grady inside, not knowing what to expect. The bar was poorly lit and as dingy and disheveled inside as outside. There were booths on the left side and a long bar on the right. Two or three locals were sitting at the bar, but the booths were empty. There were two large jars on the bar, one partially filled with pickled pigs' feet and the other partially filled with pickled eggs. We took a seat in a booth as one of the locals hollered, "Sally, give me one of them eggs!"

After a minute, a young woman came over and sat next to Grady, giving him a quick kiss on the cheek. Grady introduced her as Sally. She was a thin girl with long, blond hair flowing down her back, and she had a very pleasantly shaped face. She wore a very short dress, which was cut low at the top. Every visible portion of her body was tattooed from the neck down. Though I tried, I couldn't help staring at her tattoos. "Do you work here, Sally?" I asked.

"Yes," she answered, "and what are you staring at?"

"You have a lot of tattoos," I responded weakly.

"Yes," she said a bit defensively, "there's a tattoo parlor upstairs, and whenever I get drunk, I just go up and get another."

When we left the bar, I looked up and saw a faded sign lettered TATOOS in red paint. I never saw Sally again, but I have often wondered what would cause an attractive young girl to do such a thing to herself. When describing her to me, Grady had never mentioned that she had any tattoos.

Grady was, to say the least, an interesting friend. He had a two-year degree from a junior college in Oklahoma City but had never been able to find very satisfactory employment. He had been given the opportunity to go to Officers Candidate School and saw the life of an army officer as a great opportunity for him. He wanted to make a career of it, but he did not seem to be able to buckle down and study when it was necessary. At the end of the course, we were to take a test on weapons, which was the final exam for Infantry Officers Basic Training Course. The night before the exam, I spent a couple of hours studying and got ready to turn in early. Grady came in late, but not as late as usual, announcing that he needed to study for the exam. I went to bed, leaving him sitting at his desk, pouring over the statistics and nomenclature of the various military weapons in the army's arsenal.

An hour or so later he got up and went to the little refrigerator we had in our room and awoke me with the question, "Do we have any oranges?" I told him I didn't think we had any. After fumbling around some, he finally went to bed and cut his light off. In just a few minutes, he said, "John?"

I had almost gone back to sleep, but I answered, "Yes?"

There was a long pause before he asked, "What is the bursting radius of an M30 grenade?"

"I don't know," I answered. "Go to sleep."

A few minutes later in a sleepy voice, he softly muttered, "I sure wish I had an orange." And then in a minute or so after that, in a voice heavy with sleep, "No kidding, John, what *is* the bursting radius of an orange?"

The happy ending to the story was that Grady passed the test—although not with a stellar score. He and I, along with approximately one hundred other junior officers, graduated from the Infantry Officer's school in late June of 1968 and received our assignments, sending us to duty stations all over the United States. I was convinced then, and still believe today, that we received the best basic training available to prepare us for mortal combat.

When my training ended in June 1968, I was assigned to Company B, Second Battalion, 46th Mechanized Infantry, First Armored Division at Fort Hood in Killeen, Texas.

My company commander was a very amiable first lieutenant who had graduated from West Point Military Academy. After only two months, he left for Vietnam, and I took over as commander. I was twenty-three years old, had only been in the army for five months, and was suddenly in charge of 160 men and several million dollars worth of vehicles and equipment. I was the only company commander in the entire brigade who was a second lieutenant.

Being a company commander was the most challenging test of my life to that point. I literally had no idea how to run a mechanized infantry company. Fortunately, I was only in command for two months, and I had some very good noncommissioned officers (NCOs) under me who did their best to keep me straight. A captain, and a senior captain at that, normally held the company commander position, but officers were in short supply in 1968, and the task fell to me as a green second lieutenant.

One day when we were out in the field on an exercise, it became apparent that we needed a manual that I had left on my desk in company headquarters. Hearing this, my senior platoon sergeant, Sergeant Lumpkin, called a soldier over, saying, "Listen, I want you to run back to company headquarters and bring me the manual that is sitting on the old man's desk." Then he looked at me and said, "I mean, on the lieutenant's desk."

"Old man" was a label generally reserved for company commanders, but in my case, it was just too much of a stretch, given my young age and inexperience. Officers may have been the leaders, but it was a well-known fact that sergeants ran the army. General Dwight D. Eisenhower is reported to have said, "The sergeant is the army." As a young and inexperienced company commander, I know that I would have been lost without them.

I had two excellent first sergeants during my brief command of "B" Company. The first was an older, grizzled man who was very dissatisfied with the condition of the stateside army. I understood his frustration. In addition to being short on senior officers, we were also short on equipment, supplies, and spare parts because they were all being shipped overseas. The morale of the men was terrible because our unit was basically a holding place for soldiers who were just back from Vietnam and were only waiting for their enlistments to be finished so they could go home.

By 1968 the war had become so burdensome on the resources of the stateside military that the army had virtually become a shadow of its former self. Already I was beginning to see how this extended conflict, with no resolution in sight, was destroying the very fabric of the army. My discouraged first sergeant got a three-day pass, took a flight to D.C., and went to the Pentagon where he had himself assigned to a unit in Vietnam. One week later, he left, and his replacement arrived the next day.

My new first sergeant was a large young man, six foot five and 250 pounds. The second day on the job, he received a call from the battalion sergeant major, whom he had not yet met. The sergeant major was also a large man, probably six foot seven and 300 pounds. He berated the first sergeant over the phone for not having accomplished some written order that had been previously issued. I was working at my desk, and I looked up to see the first sergeant slam the phone down and storm out of the office muttering, "Nobody talks to me like that. I'm going up there and beat his ass."

With great difficulty I resisted the urge to go up to headquarters to watch this confrontation of these two Goliaths. Deciding that it would be best to stay put, I turned my swivel chair around so that I could watch out the window for the first sergeant's return. Very soon I saw him emerge from the headquarters building, walking slowly back down the street with his head down and his shoulders slumped forward.

I stood in the doorway of my office so that I could see his face when he reentered the orderly room. The crimson color of his complexion had been replaced with stark white, and looking at me, he said weakly, "Sir, I was going to beat his ass, but you know what? He's bigger than I am!"

It had probably never happened before. This powerful, but normally gentle, man had probably never before confronted someone who was not only senior to him in rank, but also his superior in size and strength. After that day, the first sergeant was careful to keep up with all orders that came down from battalion headquarters.

In addition to these first sergeants, I had a good cadre of platoon sergeants, and all of these senior NCOs did their best to help me survive and keep me out of trouble, but it was inevitable that I would occasionally mess up because of my lack of experience.

On one occasion, the battalion executive officer, a major, chewed me out for some mistake I had made. We were standing outside the company headquarters at the time, and when the major left, I turned to go inside with my head hanging down. Sergeant Lumpkin was standing behind me and had heard the shellacking that the major had given me. "Don't be so upset, sir," he said. "After all, you're *only* a lieutenant. You're authorized to screw up!"

I don't know why exactly, but this bit of advice from this seasoned NCO lifted my spirits and made it easier to take whatever misfortune happened to come my way while holding this awesome command responsibility.

I was at Fort Hood when Colonel Wheeler, the brigade commander, personally delivered the orders assigning me to Vietnam. The colonel came into my office without returning salutes to the company clerk or the first sergeant, walked straight to my desk with a very serious look on his face, and handed me the orders. Then he said, "I went up to headquarters to have you assigned to my staff, and they gave me your orders for Vietnam. I'm sorry. I had hoped you would have a few more months here."

I had gotten to know Colonel Wheeler fairly well. He was from Virginia, and we hit it off immediately. Whenever he needed a junior officer for field exercises, he would call for me. I had been told that the best way to advance in the army was to stay with a star, a general, and hold on to his coattails as he advanced through the system. If I had stayed in the army, I would have tried to stay with Colonel Wheeler, who interestingly enough, would become General Wheeler within a few months and go to Vietnam as a division commander. Soon after Thanksgiving 1968, I left Fort Hood headed for the East Coast again. I had gained valuable command experience and had acquired considerable confidence that I could handle whatever new assignment the army had for me.

My orders first sent me to Fort Bragg in North Carolina where I attended a course at the Special Forces School, which was meant to prepare me to be an advisor to Vietnamese combat troops as part of MACV (Military Advisory Command Vietnam). Additionally, I was selected to go to Vietnamese language school at Fort Bliss Texas.

I soon realized that I was about to become part of what President Richard Nixon's administration called "Vietnamization" of the war. It was Nixon's strategy to get us out of the war by building up the South Vietnamese forces, so they could take over the fight, and we could come home. At the time, this sounded like a good idea, but I would eventually learn that the South Vietnamese lacked the will to fight, and this strategy, therefore, was doomed to failure.

As my departure date drew nearer, I began to carefully watch the casualty figures coming out of Vietnam as recorded in the *Army Times*. When President Nixon was inaugurated, we were losing approximately 400 men per week in Vietnam. By the time I went over in May 1969 that number had dropped to about 200 per week. I felt fortunate and thought my chances of survival were improving, but I reasoned that I needed to be careful to be sure that I did not become one of the statistics.

By the time I returned home in 1970, the United States had lost a total of about 40,000 men in Vietnam. Despite Nixon's pledge to end the war, it would drag on another three years at a cost in excess of an additional 18,000 American deaths. The total number of wounded, many who were permanently disabled, would ultimately exceed 250,000. Some military historians have speculated that if we had not been blessed to have helicopters for medical evacuation, the number of deaths may have been double the eventual total of approximately 58,000. I would eventually learn first hand how this protracted conflict, with continuing significant casualties, was having a seriously adverse affect on the morale of our fighting men.

At Fort Bragg we received a refresher course on general weapons and tactics, as well as some very good training specific to Vietnam from men who had been there; some more than once. Two of these men I remember most clearly.

One was a captain who would go with my class on field exercises. We had blanks in our rifles one day when we were walking along a wooded trail at Fort Bragg. This captain was walking beside me with a long walking stick, when some yo-yo fired a blank behind us. I watched in amazement as the captain elevated himself, turned to the rear, and hit the ground with his walking stick shouldered and aiming down the trail. I recalled that incident later after I had returned home from Vietnam and was playing badminton at a friend's house in Richmond on the Fourth of July. Some neighborhood children set off firecrackers behind me, and before I could stop, I found myself on the ground, aiming the racket toward the rear. I was quite embarrassed as I looked up to see my companions staring at me in disbelief. I expected them to laugh, but they didn't.

The other officer I best remember at Fort Bragg spoke as part of a panel of senior officers at our final briefing before graduation. It was soon evident to us that this major had the most experience of anyone on the panel (three tours), and he received the majority of the questions. When asked if he had been wounded. "Six times," was his answer.

"How did it happen?" he was asked.

"Everything from a grenade, to bullets, and a knife. A little boy handed me the grenade, which was inside a bag of tea leaves. I was suspicious immediately and tried to toss it, but it still got me."

"Will you go back?" he was asked.

His answer was an emphatic, "No, I'm getting out." The fact that this man had been a combat advisor greatly increase my apprehension about what to expect once I arrived at my eventual duty station in Vietnam.

When my training was finished, I returned to West Point to tell my family and friends good-bye. Everyone greeted me warmly and said they would be happy to see me return, but there was something rather peculiar about the way they behaved. I never experienced the ridicule that some Vietnam-era soldiers complained about, but still, people treated me very strangely. It must be the way people with terminal diseases are treated. It was very awkward. They acted as though an unfortunate thing had befallen me (like cancer), and they hoped I would survive, but there was no honor or valor in it. There was one little, old lady in my hometown of West Point who was different. She seemed to appreciate the sacrifice I was about to make for my country. One day when I bumped into her in the A&P grocery store, she said with a snaggle-toothed grin, "Kill a couple for me, will you?" I returned her smile and said that I would do my best.

* *not to scale*

CHAPTER 2

ARRIVAL IN COUNTRY (VIETNAM)

*We of the Kennedy and Johnson administrations who partici-
pated in the decisions on Vietnam acted according to what we
thought were the principles and traditions of this nation. We
made our decisions in light of those values. Yet we were terribly
wrong.*

—Robert S. McNamara,
In Retrospect: The Tragedy and Lessons of Vietnam (1995)

The flight from Dulles Airport in D.C. took me to Los Angeles where I boarded
a bus and rode to Oakland. The flight from Oakland to Vietnam took sixteen
hours and we stopped briefly in Alaska and Japan. We did not have time to
leave either airport, but I remember a large, stuffed grizzly bear at the terminal
in Anchorage. It was fierce looking, standing on its hind legs with arms outstretched, and I saw the bear as a symbol of things to come because of its
power, ferocity, and threat of danger.

I don't remember much about the flight except it being long and tiresome. I
do remember the landing at Tan Son Nhat Airport in Saigon. The pilot warned
us that he would descend rapidly to avoid ground fire, and as the plane banked
heavily and headed for the end of the runway, I saw artillery rounds (ours, I

presumed) landing in the jungle outside the city. I knew at that moment that this was the war, and it was real. I would soon learn that I was going to be part of an ancient struggle that had been raging on the land below for centuries.

The Vietnamese culture is an old one, dating back a couple of thousand years, with a history of conflict stretching back to its beginning. Over the last 2,000 years, the Vietnamese people have fought for their independence against China, Cambodia, and the French, who occupied the country from 1863 until 1940 when the Japanese expelled them and set up a puppet government.

During World War II, Ho Chi Minh and his deputy, General Vo Nguyen Giap, led a resistance effort against the Japanese that was supported by the Allies. After World War II, the French tried to reassert their control but were eventually run out of the country in 1954 by a Communist force headed by Ho Chi Minh with strong support from Russia and China.

Upon the departure of the French, the country was divided at the 17th parallel into North Vietnam under Ho Chi Minh and South Vietnam with strong ties to the West. After the division of the country, the Communists in the North immediately began to try to reunite the country by supporting a guerilla insurgency force in the South called the National Liberation Front (NLF) but more commonly known by our side as the Vietcong or the VC.

Under the terms of the 1954 peace accords, there were supposed to be elections to reunite the country, but they never took place reportedly because the Eisenhower administration feared that Ho Chi Minh would win. The Vietcong began attacking the South Vietnamese forces as well as other government officials, such as, village chiefs. The United States became involved in the conflict in the early 1960s in an effort to help the South Vietnamese defeat the Vietcong and their allies, the North Vietnamese Army (NVA). Russia and Red China supplied the North Vietnamese and the VC with arms, ammunition, and other supplies.

The United States' involvement grew from a small advisory effort in 1962 to a contingency of more than 500,000 U.S. soldiers in country by 1968. Likewise the Russians and the Chinese increased their involvement by supplying vast amounts of supplies, arms, ammunition, and advisors. We now know that the Chinese actually deployed thousands of engineers and troops inside North Vietnam during this period for the purpose of rebuilding railroads, bridges, highways, and factories that had been destroyed by American bombing.

For the most part, the U.S. military effort was successful from a purely military point of view. By 1968, the South Vietnamese and U.S. forces controlled most of the population centers in the South, and the VC and NVA were confined to small pockets in the jungle and in camps set up in Cambodia and Laos. From these camps, the enemy would launch attacks against villages, U.S. posts, and even the large cities, such as, Saigon.

The strategy of the North, as espoused by General Giap, was based upon its willingness to suffer great casualties in order to achieve their objectives in the face of superior U.S. firepower. Over time they hoped to wear us down so that we would eventually give up and leave. The strategy worked. By the end of the war, the American people were outraged that we had lost almost 58,000 people. By comparison, the NVA/VC are thought to have sacrificed around 1,200,000 lives, while the South lost around 600,000.

Except for a few small engagements, the United States won every major battle of consequence. Even the famous Tet Offensive of January 1968, which is thought to be the turning point when the American people began to lose confidence, was actually a resounding military defeat for the VC. However our press never reported the complete story and dwelt, instead, on the limited and short-lived successes of the enemy. The week of the battle, Walter Cronkite reported on the *CBS Evening News* that "it seems now more certain than ever that the bloody experience of Vietnam is to end in a stalemate."

In any other war this battle would have been reported as a magnificent victory. The historical fact is that NVA/VC losses during the Tet Offensive were staggering, with entire units being wiped out or reduced to the point where they were ineffective. Enemy losses were put at 37,000; American deaths were reported at only about 2,500. Despite the lopsided U.S. victory, the reaction of the American people was so negative that by March of that year the percentage of Americans who approved of President Johnson's conduct of the war had fallen to only 26 percent. Johnson announced on March 31, 1968, that he would not seek another term.

Despite our military successes, we were doomed to lose the larger conflict because our stated aim after 1968 was to strengthen the South Vietnamese so that they could eventually take over their own defense and repel the North. This would never happen because the people of the South were never interested in preserving their independence, while the North Vietnamese and the VC fought with great vigor and determination to reunite their country and drive out the "Imperial Invaders."

Complete military victory was further prevented by the U.S. policy that strictly limited U.S. military operations to South Vietnamese soil. Lt. Gen. Harold Moor (U.S. Army ret.), the co-author of the highly acclaimed book *We Were Soldiers Once…and Young*, laments not being able to pursue the enemy after the battle of Ia Drang in 1965. In his final chapter, entitled Reflections and Perceptions, Moor quotes Brigadier General Douglas Kinnard (ret), Moor's commander at the time of the battle, as saying, "I was always taught as an officer that in a pursuit situation you continue to pursue until you either kill the enemy or he surrenders. I saw the Ia Drang as a definite pursuit situation and I wanted to keep after them. Not to follow them into Cambodia violated every principle of warfare. I was supported in this by both the military and civilian leaders in Siagon. But the decision was made back there, at the White House, that we would not be permitted to pursue into Cambodia. It became perfectly clear to the North Vietnamese that they then had sanctuary; they could come when they were ready to fight and leave when they were ready to quit." As an advisor, I would soon become painfully aware of this problem and would eventually have to decide whether to violate this prohibition and accomplish the mission or respect it and fail.

By 1969 the American military emphasis was beginning to shift from one of amassing as much enemy body count as possible, to preparing the Vietnamese military to take over the war. The effort was referred to as "Vietnamization," and I was to become part of it.

At the same time, regular American Army infantry units were becoming involved in a program that was called "Pacification." Under this program, company or platoon-sized units were placed in defensive positions next to villages out in the countryside. These American units were to provide security to the area by keeping the VC at bay so that the people could go about their normal activities without being intimidated or harassed. This effort was only marginally successful because in many of these areas, a large number of the people were VC sympathizers as well as family of the VC soldiers who were operating in the area.

Platoon Leader, by James R. McDonough, is an excellent book that depicts an American rifle platoon performing this pacification function in Binh Dinh Province. In his book, McDonough describes efforts, which were both heroic and well executed, by his platoon to accomplish this mission, but which would prove to be ineffective. In chapter 4 he laments, "The enemy was of the people here in Binh Dinh province. They were, in every respect, indistinguishable from the peasantry. There was no way to separate the two. The village people were their family. All the barbed wire, all the curfews, all the military presence in the world, could not sever the ties between them."

I spent two days in Saigon before receiving my orders, which were to join a mobile advisory team in Tay Ninh Province. While awaiting my assignment in

Saigon, I spent most of the time at the Officers Club. One day while there, I noticed some graffiti written on the bathroom wall, which had a profound effect on my thinking. It said, "Vietnam is the Edsel of American foreign policy." For those who might be too young to know, the Edsel was a very ugly automobile produced by Ford in the early 1960s. That car was a terrible flop, but useful for that analogy.

Before traveling to Tay Ninh, I was sent to Bien Hoa for two more weeks of training. The training at Bien Hoa was mostly a repeat of what I had already learned at Fort Bragg and was of little value. The only thing that I learned that would come in handy later, came from a first lieutenant one night at the Officers Club who said, "If you ever have to take a tree line that might hold VC, about the only thing you can do is line all of your men up and go in with everyone firing, hoping you will scare the hell out of any VC who might be there." I stored this knowledge in the back of my mind as a bit of advice that later would prove to be useful.

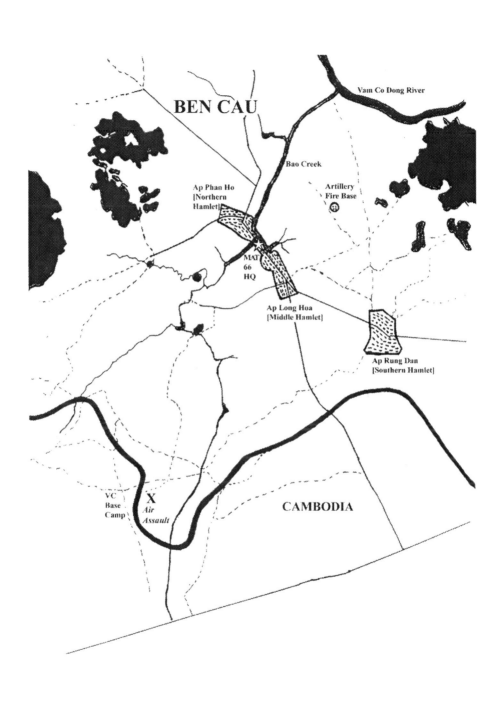

On his first day in Tay Ninh Province, the author was greeted at the airstrip by two Red Cross jeeps, each containing bodies of Vietnamese soldiers who had been killed in combat. There was also a truck full of wounded Vietnamese soldiers who were waiting for transport to the hospital. This was the first of many dead and wounded soldiers that he would see during his stay in Tay Ninh.

As Americans, we are appalled that we lost approximately 58,000 soldiers in the Vietnam War, but we forget, or never knew, that the South Vietnamese lost close to 600,000 people in the war and that the North Vietnamese and the Vietcong lost close to 1.2 million.

CHAPTER 3

BEN CAU

For waging war you need guidance,
and for victory many advisers.

—The Holy Bible, Proverbs 24:6 (NIV)

Following the two weeks of training at Bien Hoa, I boarded a small, single-engine plane that took me to Tay Ninh City, which lies close to the Vam Co Dong River (Song Vam Co Dong) and next to the Nui Ba Dinh, the Black Virgin Mountain. The actual translation is Black Lady Mountain but Virgin seems to have become more popular, especially for American tourists. This mountain is the most prominent feature in the whole province, and there are several legends about how it got its name. They all involve a young Vietnamese princess of ancient times who died tragically because of lost love. Aptly, the lost lover is generally depicted in the legend as a young soldier.

After landing on a rather crude runway on the west side of the mountain, I stepped from the plane and looked around, but could see nothing that looked army except a small sandbag bunker beside the runway. I walked to it and rapped sharply on the crude wooden door. An army special forces captain wearing a green beret came to the door. I snapped to attention, saluted, and said, "Lieutenant Loving reporting for duty, sir." He gave me an amused look and stepped out without returning the salute. He pointed toward a large, old

French masonry building on the other side of the runway and told me to report there.

After wandering around for some time in the old building, I found the commanding officer, Colonel Cloud, who welcomed me and told me that I should catch a helicopter that afternoon that would take me to a small village called Ben Cau in the western part of the province. I would later learn that Ben Cau translates as Bridge Port in English. It was necessary to fly, he explained, because the roads to that part of the province were not secure. I would be second in command of Mobile Advisory Team (MAT) 66 that was part of Advisory Team 90, Tay Ninh Province.

While waiting on the runway for the chopper, I noticed that there were two jeeps beside the runway. Each contained two bodies wrapped tightly in rubber ponchos, their round, green heads visible inside of each jeep. I didn't know whether they were Vietnamese or American, but I assumed they were Vietnamese because they were small in stature. Later I learned that this was how the Vietnamese cared for their dead in the field; Americans used body bags. It was a rather gruesome introduction to my new assignment but appropriate because I would eventually see a number of young Vietnamese men brought to this state before my tour was over. There was also a truck loaded with wounded South Vietnamese soldiers.

The helicopter ride to Ben Cau was short. Whenever I took these flights across the countryside, I was always amazed at the pot marks that dotted the land. They were huge bomb craters from B52 bombers that flew every night and dropped thousands of pounds of ordnance on the land below, hoping to hit the enemy. Almost every night I spent in Tay Ninh Province, I felt my bunk shake from the explosions of this air campaign.

Despite the bomb craters, it was a beautiful part of the country. Everything was green. Our bombs and artillery tore great, brown holes in the green fabric, but the land healed itself quickly, like a large, green lizard that grows new appendages when lost. Fertile rice patties were laid out in neat squares all along the river, which snaked through the countryside like a long, blue ribbon. The mountain sat roughly in the middle of the province next to Tay Ninh, the "Holy City," while the river flowed around it from northwest to southeast, feeding the rice paddies with water and providing transportation and fish for the people. The southern part of the province was mostly rice paddies with small patches of woods; while the northern part, which was called War Zone C, was mostly jungle, grassland, and bamboo.

Ben Cau was located in an area of Vietnam called the "Angels Wing" because it stuck out into Cambodia, looking like the wing of an angel on the map. The village was very close to the Cambodian border in an area that was notorious as a VC stronghold. The infamous Ho Chi Minh Trail, which originated in North Vietnam and ran south through Laos and Cambodia, actually terminated in this area of Tay Ninh Province. Most of the men, material, and supplies that fueled the Vietcong insurgency came down this trail from the north to the south.

Ben Cau was actually made up of three small villages, or hamlets, with the seat of control, group headquarters, in the middle hamlet next to the bridge. The headquarters building was a crude, wooden structure with a tin roof, which, I noted from the air, was full of holes caused by mortar rounds or rockets. The other two villages also had a South Vietnamese company assigned to each for security. This was an effective method of securing the rural areas against the activities of the VC in the countryside, working very well as a defense against small VC forces and occasional attacks from North Vietnamese Army units passing through the area. The government troops were called Regional Forces but were manned with soldiers from all over, especially Saigon.

Mobile Advisory Team 66 was assigned with the Regional Forces to provide support and advice. The support, I would discover, amounted mostly to calling in firepower from artillery and helicopter gunships, as well as bringing in medical helicopters called "dust-offs" or "medevacs" to evacuate the wounded. Another, unofficial support activity was helping the Vietnamese troops obtain certain supplies and munitions. At first, the advisory function seemed a bit presumptuous to me since our counterpart Vietnamese officers had generally been fighting for years and had more experience with war than I would ever have. However, I would soon learn that the thing that we could never give our counterparts was the will to fight. They fought because they had to, while their enemies, the VC and the North Vietnamese regulars, fought with a burning desire, fueled by nationalism, to unite their country and rid it of foreign influence.

When we reached Ben Cau, the chopper sat down on a grassy spot next to the river just below the bridge. The waterway at this spot was actually a tributary of the great Vam Co Dong River (Song Vam Co Dong) named Rach Bao, and the bridge marked the end of the navigable stream. A young, blond-haired, mustachioed, American lieutenant, who welcomed me warmly, exclaimed that I must be his replacement and said that he was sure glad to see me.

He led me to the team's headquarters, which was across the bridge on the other side of the river. As we crossed the bridge he said, "I'm going home in two weeks, and now that you're here, I'm not leaving the bunker until that big chopper comes to take me away." I am sorry that I don't remember the lieutenant's name, but he was a rather likable fellow. I'll call him Lieutenant "Short" since "short" was our term for a man who would be going home soon. He talked a lot about going home and told me about this airline stewardess he had met in Los Angeles before leaving for Vietnam. He said he had never been able to get her off his mind, and the first thing he would do when he landed in the States was to try to find her. During the next two weeks, he only left our large, sandbag bunker once, a decision he would later regret.

As we entered the compound, I noticed it was heavily fortified, with a berm and a moat all around the perimeter, which was surrounded by coils of barbed wire and razor wire. There were fighting positions and machine gun bunkers placed on all sides. Unlike most forts in Vietnam, which were triangular in shape, this one was a rectangle with clear fields of fire on all sides and enfilade fire from the corners. I would later learn that the perimeter had numerous mines and booby traps sprinkled among the coils of wire.

Before the day was over, I met all of the members of Mobile Advisory Team 66. First I met Captain Smith, who was the senior advisor and head of the team. He was a thin man in his early thirties. When we met, he was sitting in a chair inside the bunker, wearing only his underwear and a pair of flip-flops. I saluted and extended my hand to him. He shook my hand but I don't believe he ever stood up. I soon learned that he spent most of his time in that chair, reading paperback Westerns. If he ever got up and put on his fatigues, you knew he was going into Tay Ninh, which he did about once a week.

Captain Smith was a quiet man who had very little to say and gave the rest of us no trouble. He never said anything about his experiences in Vietnam, but I knew he was in the second half of his second tour and that he had won the Bronze Star with "V" for valor. By the time I arrived in Ben Cau, it was pretty much understood that he had already done his time in the field and was not expected to go out on operations. This was fine with me, and I did not resent him for it at all. He told me that day that two of the American members of our team went on operations with the Vietnamese soldiers about every day. That meant that we other four members would alternate going out approximately every other day. He said that I should plan to go out the next day.

Next I met Sergeant First Class Melvin Davis, who was called Dave, the senior NCO on the team. He was forty years old and had a wife and seven children in Florida. He was one of the finest men I have ever known. He was the heavy-weapons expert, a small, wiry black man who looked after the rest of us and kept things running smoothly. Dave was serving his second tour in Vietnam and was a veteran of Korea. He had put in papers to retire after twenty-years service but had been sent back for another tour after his retirement had been delayed.

The light-weapons expert was Sergeant First Class Mack Rice, who was called Mack, and was also black. Mack was in his mid-twenties and was a very capable NCO. He was serving his second tour also and had learned quite a bit about Vietnam and the war. He supplied us with most of our food by making regular trips into the 25th Infantry Division base camp and returning with loads of *free* frozen food. I wondered how he did this when I knew that we were supposed to buy our food from the PX.

Later I happened to be with him when he made one of these trips, and I discovered his secret. He went to the headquarters mess hall at one of the companies in the 25th Infantry Division and asked for a certain mess sergeant. "He's gone," was the response, "rotated last week." A worried look came to Mack's face as he asked to see the departed sergeant's replacement. The new mess sergeant turned out to be a rather friendly sort, and Mack quickly began an easy conversation with him. Mack told him we were stationed out in the boonies with the Vietnamese troops on dangerous duty with only five of us Americans to look out for each other. Eventually came the key question from our new friend, the mess sergeant, "But how do you guys eat out there?"

Mack looked down at his feet. "Well, Sarge, that fish and rice gets really old."

The mess sergeant immediately rose, went to his large walk-in freezer and threw open the door. "Take what you need, Sarge," he said.

Our medic was a specialist E4 named Skeeter, who was twenty-one years old from northern New York State. He drank too much, and I was not sorry to see him go when it was his turn to rotate. In his defense, however, he took his turn going on operations and never complained about it even though he was not really trained for combat. I didn't trust him and never took him on operations when I expected trouble.

Each six-man mobile advisory team was assigned a Vietnamese interpreter. Our interpreter was a Vietnamese sergeant named Bock. Bock was probably the tallest Vietnamese I ever met, being about my height at six feet. He was a devout Catholic who was born in North Vietnam. The VC had killed his parents, so he came South as a young man. He was well educated and his English was excellent. Although the American members of the team rotated operation assignments, the interpreter went out each time. Bock was transferred soon after I arrived and replaced by a young man named Nea.

The last person I met was Captain Tail, who was our Vietnamese counterpart and group commander of the three companies stationed at Ben Cau. He was about average height for a Vietnamese but a bit stockier than the average. He had a very ruddy complexion, which looked like the remnants of a serious skin disease. I estimated his age at somewhere between thirty-five and forty. I would eventually learn that this officer was a bit of a paradox, as were most of the Vietnamese we advised, being that he was fairly aggressive and conscientious. I would eventually learn, however, that he had faults as well as strengths. I'm sure that if he is alive today and writing his memoir, he would say the same about me.

Once I entered Ben Cau, I assumed a new role. I was no longer John, or even Lieutenant Loving. I became *Trung uy*, which means "first lieutenant" in Vietnamese. Even the other Americans on the team would call me this, and with the new name I would face new challenges.

Just a couple of years before, I had been barely more than a boy. Suddenly I had become a soldier, and then an officer, and then I was the "old man," leading a company of men in Texas. Now I would assume this new role of leading men in combat. I would be responsible for them. If they got hurt or killed, it would be my responsibility. More than this, I would be the Trung uy whom my Vietnamese counterparts would look to for advice, guidance, and support. I would be expected to be calm under fire, to make the right decisions under stress, and to do my duty whatever the cost. I had received the best possible training. I had the best equipment and firepower in the world at my disposal, but I wondered if I would personally measure up. In my mind I questioned if I could really, fully make the transition from man-boy to combat leader.

Regional Forces company headquarters at Ben Cau as viewed from the open door of a helicopter. The wooden building to the left of center housed the Vietnamese Regional Forces group headquarters. Its new tin roof was made necessary because of many holes in the old roof, resulting from numerous VC mortar attacks.

The low, gray structure in the middle of the compound is the sandbag bunker shared by Mobile Advisory Team (MAT) 66 and the Vietnamese group commander, Captain Tail. The concrete obelisk monument between the company street and the moat was the spot where one of our men was seriously wounded when his rocket launcher unexpectedly exploded as he sat it down on the edge of the monument.

Three Vietnamese junior officers at Ben Cau with the author, second from right. This picture was taken inside the Regional Forces group headquarters building. During enemy attacks, the stretchers in the right-hand corner were used to retrieve the dead and wounded. This building was not fortified in any way and was a very dangerous place to be during mortar attacks. It was apparent that the location of this building had been precisely recorded by VC spies and was, therefore, a favorite target.

CHAPTER 4

FIRST OPERATION

We are not about to send
American boys 9 or 10,000 miles
away from home to do what
Asian boys ought to be doing for themselves.

—Lyndon Baines Johnson
Speech at Akron University
October 21, 1964

The day after my arrival in Ben Cau, I went on my first operation. Operation orders came in each night over the radio in code. They generally called for a reconnaissance patrol out into the surrounding countryside. We would decode the message and then plot out the route of the patrol on a map that we would take with us the next day. I kept my map inside a plastic bag and drew the route of march on the plastic cover with a grease pencil.

A typical, simple operation would involve a platoon-sized force (about twenty men), which would be sent out on an eight- to ten-kilometer hike to look for VC activity in the area. A more complicated operation would involve a company of sixty to eighty men or a group of 150 men in a force, which might be picked up and returned by helicopters.

With the larger forces, we would be on a "search and destroy mission," which was usually directed at some specific location or against enemy forces suspected to be in the area. All of these units were under-strength. A full-sized rifle company should consist of 160 men, but units in both the U.S. Army and the South Vietnamese Army were almost never up to this strength. A typical U.S. company would more likely consist of 100 to 120 operational men; whereas, a typical South Vietnamese company was more likely to field between sixty and one hundred men.

I carried an M16 rifle on these operations as did most of the other men on the patrol. Additionally I carried a bag containing twelve to fifteen clips of ammunition, a U.S. Navy Mark 2 knife with a seven-inch blade, and a Swiss Army knife.

The Swiss Army knife was useful, but the large knife saw little action except for one day near the end of my tour when I was very happy to have it. At other times, its use was limited. I was able to throw this knife into a tree at any dis tance between six and twelve feet, an accomplishment that was of limited value except to entertain the troops during breaks while on operations.

My Vietnamese counterpart officers carried either 38-caliber or 45-caliber pistols. I was offered a pistol when I arrived in Saigon, but I opted, instead, for the rifle because of its superior firepower and range. One of the men would usually carry an M60 machine gun and another would carry an M79 grenade launcher. Several of the men would usually carry LAWs (light antitank weapons) in addition to their rifles. A LAW was a very light, short tube with a sight set along the top. It could be extended and fired from the shoulder at heavily fortified positions. It acted like the old Bazooka, firing a powerful, armor-piercing rocket that could knock out a tank if deployed properly.

I was trained at Forts Benning and Bragg on all of these weapons plus the 50-caliber machine gun, the Thompson machine gun, and the 81mm and 60mm mortars. I qualified as an expert with both the M16 rifle and the 45-caliber pistol. As an advisor, I was expected to be able to train my Vietnamese counterparts and their troops in the use of all of these weapons.

There was a lot of discussion about the reliability of the U.S. M16 rifle versus the enemy AK47 rifle, which was produced in Russia. The most widely held opinion was that the AK47 was a vastly superior weapon. I, frankly, wasn't sure. I fired both weapons and felt more at ease with the M16 and seemed to be able to shoot more accurately with the M16, but the AK47 did seem to be more stoutly built and more durable. Many soldiers reported that their M16s jammed during heavy use, and I do remember seeing a pile of dilapidated-looking M16s at the armory in Saigon. I was told that they had been turned in for refurbishing. I never had a problem with my personal weapon and never saw one that had jammed among our Vietnamese troops.

My first operation was a platoon-sized reconnaissance patrol and was uneventful, just like scores that I would go on during my tour. First Lt. Kan, a Vietnamese officer in his early forties, which was old for a junior officer, led the patrol from the outpost in the southern village. We left the perimeter of our fort at about 0800 headed in a roughly northwest direction. As we moved out, I was immediately impressed with the natural beauty of the country. Tay Ninh Province had a nice combination of all the terrain found in the South. It contained lots of rice paddies but also fair amounts of jungle, scrubland, and bamboo areas. The river meandered lazily in a north to south direction, its banks dotted with fishing huts and palm trees.

As we walked, I saw men and women working in the fields, which were tilled and ready for planting. The weather was very hot and humid with occasional afternoon rains at that time of year. After a short walk across rice paddy dikes, we picked up a path that wound through a medium-sized patch of jungle and came out not far from our village base camp.

As we moved along, I was very aware of the hot, almost stifling, heavy air and began to sweat profusely. After about two hours, the Vietnamese lieutenant leading the patrol halted for a rest. I sat down on a log beside a Vietnamese soldier and breathed heavily, sweat pouring off me. The soldier looked at me and said, "*Trung uy mat qua*," which meant "the lieutenant is too fat." At six feet tall I only weighed 165 pounds, but for this climate, he was right. I answered, "*Ya, Trung uy mat qua.*" He smiled happily at hearing me speak his language.

When we reached somewhere near the middle of the forest, the point man tripped a wire that set off a loud whistling flair. We were all startled, and I stood frozen for a moment, waiting for an explosion that didn't come. I knew immediately it couldn't be a booby trap because there would be no warning. After much discussion among the Vietnamese, Bock told me that an American long-range reconnaissance patrol (LRRP) had spent the night in these woods and had probably put out the flares to warn them of any approach by the VC in the dark.

As we moved along, more wires were tripped and whistles sounded, making everyone very nervous. After awhile, I noticed that Lt. Kan had moved past his forward men and was now walking point. I was right behind him. "Bock," I said, "tell Trung uy that he is not supposed to walk point. Soldiers are supposed to walk point." Bock passed on what I said, and the response back was,

"Sometimes a leader must lead." This "old" lieutenant would eventually show me that he was a true paradox, a man who would vary from being ambivalent to being a man of courage and cunning.

We eventually made it out of the forest, and thus ended my first operation, relatively uneventful, and what was for me a fairly pleasant hike through the beautiful Vietnam countryside. As we walked out of the woods, I thought to myself that this actually felt fairly natural. It reminded me of the many days I had spent back home in Virginia, walking through the woods with a shotgun or a rifle on my shoulder, hunting squirrels, rabbits, and quail. There would be many operations to come. Most would be uneventful like this one, but others would be more exciting and eventful. Some would be more than just exciting; they would be laced with moments of terror. In those instances, the excellent training I had received would pay off handsomely.

On my second day at Ben Cau, I flew on the work chopper into district headquarters in Go Dau Ha with Capt. Smith and Dave. I met our district commander, a major who was a large man. I never liked or respected him as a leader, for reasons I'll discuss later. When we left district headquarters, we drove our jeep back to Tay Ninh on Highway No. 22, which was a well-paved road. As we passed a village, someone from the village shot at us with a rifle. I distinctly heard the bullet whiz through the air just above our heads. I was driving the jeep and, foolishly, I ducked, letting my foot off the gas pedal. Capt. Smith slapped me on the arm and yelled, "Don't slow down, fool. Speed up!"

I pressed the pedal to the floor and yelled back, "Did somebody shoot at us?"

"You're damn right, they did," was the answer. "Get us out of here fast." So I learned another lesson, which was if you're shot at while in a vehicle, don't wait around for the next shot. It was only my third day in Tay Ninh Province, and I had already been shot at by a sniper. I hoped that this was not an omen of things to come.

The bridge at Ben Cau. Ben Cau translates as Bridge Port and it was at the end of the navigable waters that flowed into Bao Dinh Creek, which was a branch of the Vam Co Dong River (Song Vam Co Dong). Since there were no good roads between Ben Cau and Tay Ninh City, this waterway was the best way to travel in and out of the area. Boats like the one showed here regularly made the trip, carrying goods and passengers. The MAT 66 team made the trip by helicopter since travel on the river would have been susceptible to ambush.

CHAPTER 5

A PARTY FOR THE DEPARTING CAPTAIN

*Older men declare war. But it is
youth who must fight and die.*

—Herbert Hoover
Republican National Convention,
Chicago, June 27, 1944

After I had been at Ben Cau for about a week, we received an invitation from Captain Tail, who had just taken over as group commander, to attend a going-away party for the former commander, Captain Trang, who was being promoted to Province S3, operations officer, at headquarters in Tay Ninh City. The invitation came to us through Bock, who assured us it would be a lavish affair that we should not miss.

The next evening at about 1600 hours, Captain Smith, Lieutenant "Short," Mack, Bock, and I eagerly walked across the bridge to a little restaurant in the village to the northeast. Dave, who did not care very much for this type of socializing, stayed in the bunker to man the radio, and Skeeter, the medic, was not around for some reason.

The restaurant was in a very modest building with a low tin roof. We took our seats at a long table that filled the room. In addition to the five men from our team, there were seven or eight Vietnamese officers and senior NCOs sitting around the table. The departing Vietnamese Captain Trang sat at the head of the table. He was a good-looking man in his late thirties, slim and of medium build. Captain Tail, Dai uy Tail in Vietnamese, sat next to him at the head of the table. I was seated between Mack and Bock. Before the food was brought out, Dai uy Tail stood and made a few remarks and then yielded the floor to Dai uy Trang who also made a few remarks and then sat down. Since this was all in Vietnamese, we did not understand much of it.

Soon the proprietress of the restaurant came out, holding a live duck and chicken, which she presented to the guest of honor, Capt. Trang, who gave each a small squeeze and pronounced them fit. Mack turned to me and said, "Now she will take them outside to kill and cook them." While the fowl were cooking, the woman came back and placed two large bowls in the middle of the table, one containing fresh green salad and the other, slightly smaller, containing eggs in the shell. She then walked around the room, speaking to the men in a very flirtatious manner. When she got to our side of the table, Bock introduced me as the new American lieutenant. Smiling she said, "*Trung uy dep try*," which translated as "the lieutenant is a pretty boy."

"*Ba dep qua. Toi sou*," I responded, meaning "Madam is very pretty, but I am ugly." This remark brought much laughter from the other men in the room and caused the woman, who was not beautiful, to smile broadly.

Lieutenant "Short" spoke out loudly above the laughter, "Not a *Ba*. She is too young. She is a *Co*." This meant "young woman." This produced more laughter as the young lieutenant reached out and took three eggs from the bowl.

After more good-natured ribbing and more laughter, we all began to serve ourselves salad and eggs. I watched as Lieutenant "Short" broke the first of his eggs. A small, well-formed, but unborn chick slid out in a gooey heap on his plate. "Ugh!" he shouted in disgust as he pushed his plate away. The whole room became silent as all eyes turned on the young lieutenant. "That's disgusting," he blurted out as everyone looked on, horrified. We were horrified by the spectacle of this unborn but recognizable little fowl, but I also realized immediately that our hosts were equally horrified by what they must have considered an unruly affront to their hospitality.

Bock spoke to me in a quiet but strained voice as the others looked on, "What is wrong? Does the lieutenant not like?"

"No" I said, "the lieutenant does not like." Captain Tail spoke next in a harsh tone to Bock, and then Bock translated, saying "We do not understand.

This is the best we have." Realizing this must be a delicacy for the Vietnamese and that it was a great sacrifice in a poor land to incubate a chicken to this point and then terminate it just before birth, I could see a small diplomatic crisis in the making.

All of the Vietnamese in the room were staring daggers at us. Thinking about what I had learned of the Vietnamese culture, I remembered their diversity of religion and their tolerance for different beliefs. On an impulse I said, "It is against our religion to eat eggs prepared this way." Bock immediately translated, where upon Captain Tail and the others nodded their heads in understanding and seemed to accept this explanation without any animosity. Lieutenant "Short," seemingly oblivious to the consternation he had caused, put back his two unbroken eggs and the happy mood resumed. Our Vietnamese hosts devoured the rest of the eggs, and we Americans enjoyed the salad.

About midway through the meal, I heard a loud explosion outside. Looking up from my plate, I turned to my right to ask Mack what it was, but he was no longer there. I looked across the room to see everyone scrambling to get through the door, and I felt Bock brush against my shoulder as he went past me to join them. I jumped up and ran across the room, finding a logjam of people trying to get through the door. Vaguely aware that more explosions were occurring outside, I finally broke through to find everyone trying to squeeze into a small sandbag bunker near the front door. Capt. Smith seemed to occupy the last available space, crouching in the entrance.

Mack and Lieutenant "Short" went out into the street, and as I followed, I saw mortar rounds landing all around. We began to run toward the river with Mack in the lead. I followed, thinking that under the bridge would be a good place to hide. About half way down the distance from the dirt road to the river, a mortar round landed in front of Mack and Lieutenant "Short." They both halted abruptly and turned, running back up the hill and almost knocking me down.

As they passed me, Mack yelled, "I'm going back to our bunker." Not having a better plan, I followed as he ran back up the little hill, down the dirt road, and onto the bridge. As we ran across the bridge, its wooden planks thumping, a Vietnamese man wearing a white shirt and black pants passed us on a bicycle. As he sped across the bridge, a mortar round landed beside him, throwing him and the bicycle about ten feet through the air. When I got to him, I stopped and knelt down beside him. He had serious wounds to both legs. Two Vietnamese soldiers who had been running behind us scooped him up, and we all ran into our fort. Once inside our bunker, I found Mack and Lt. "Short," puffing and blowing. "That was a close one!" exclaimed Lt. "Short." "I knew I should have never left the bunker."

That day was my first exposure to enemy indirect fire, and I learned several things from it. First, that the VC were experts at using the mortar. I soon learned that it was, in fact, their weapon of choice because it allowed them to inflict maximum damage while remaining at a distance. Secondly, I learned that the VC had excellent intelligence and probably knew more about our activities than I would have liked. Thirdly, I learned the sound of incoming mortar fire, and that it meant I should act fast and get down or behind cover. Even today I can hardly resist the urge to hit the ground when a truck backfires on the street.

Fortunately none of the people on our team were hurt although several Vietnamese soldiers and civilians were killed or severely wounded. We sent the wounded to the hospital via medical helicopters. This was the first time I had seen wounded people, and I was greatly moved by their suffering. Later, as I saw more wounded people, I still felt compassion for them, but I lost most of the emotion and began to accept it as a normal consequence of the war.

The mortar and artillery explosions you see in the movies are usually nothing like the real thing. The movie versions usually involve a lot of fire and smoke. The real thing involves very little visible fire, but throws lots of dirt, metal, debris, and smoke into the air, and makes a sound that is unmistakable. It sounds like a great hammer is being slammed into the earth, which shakes the very bones inside your body.

Dai uy Tail estimated that we received between fifty and sixty mortar rounds that afternoon. I had not quite finished my first week at Ben Cau and already I had been fired upon by a sniper and had been caught out in the open during a mortar attack. My chances for a quiet tour in Vietnam seemed highly unlikely.

It was customary for each mobile advisory team to hire a local woman to cook and clean for the team. Ours, who was affectionately called Mama-san, was well paid by Vietnamese standards and knew how to cook American-style food. Each day she would arrive at 0630 hours with fresh vegetables she had purchased in the market. We were supposed to purchase our meat and canned goods from the PX in Saigon, but, for the most part, it was "scrounged" from American units at the 25th Infantry Division base camp. Sergeant First Class Mack Rice was particularly adept at "scrounging" these supplies.

CHAPTER 6

MOSQUITOES AND RATS

My subject is War, and the pity of War.
The Poetry is in the pity.

—Wilfred Owen
Preface to *Poems* (1963)

Another lesson, which involved mosquitoes and rats, also came to me early in my stay at Ben Cau. The first night in the bunker, I climbed onto my cot, which was an upper bunk, lowered the mosquito netting that was draped over the upper frame, and drifted off to sleep with one of the two rotating fans blowing across me, making the heat relatively bearable. After a few minutes, Dave went outside and cut off the generator, plunging the bunker into darkness and ending the cooling breeze from the fan. I soon felt the heat fall across me like a hot, moist blanket.

Despite the heat, our bunker was a fairly comfortable place. It measured about fourteen feet by fourteen feet and had a concrete floor. Of course, the walls were constructed with sandbags to a height of about seven feet, and the roof was composed of corrugated steel with two layers of sandbags on top. There were two doors, one at the front that had strings of oriental beads hanging over the opening, and the other was to the side and opened into Captain Tail's quarters.

The interior was furnished with a wooden folding table in the center of the room capable of seating six or seven people in folding chairs. Six bunk beds were placed around the perimeter, three up and three down. There was a small gas stove and small gas refrigerator in one corner of the room with a portable wooden cabinet for pots and pans and a large, metal pan for washing dishes on a small table nearby.

Water was supplied from several large, green army water cans that were replenished every three or four days by a Vietnamese man who purported to have clean water from a local well. He sold it for a few pennies per can. As a matter of caution, we added a healthy dose of iodine tablets to each can as it was refilled because the local water was notorious for making Americans deathly ill. The ants were ferocious, even getting into our refrigerator despite its cold temperature, and the rats came out each night, roaming around the floor of the bunker, looking for morsels of food.

Every night we cranked up the generator, cut on the lights and read or watched our little black-and-white television, or played pinochle. The activity of choice generally seemed to be pinochle since the television carried only reruns, like *Star Trek*, and since there wasn't much to read. Lights went out every night at about 2200 and we were all up by 0600 or 0700, depending on what was happening that day. We had a Mama-san who came each day and served us a breakfast of eggs, bacon, ham, and toast. Two of us would then go out on the operation for the day, one would go into headquarters on the supply chopper, and the other two would find something to do inside the fort.

Except for the insecurity of being out in the countryside next to the Cambodian border in the midst of the Ho Chi Minh Trail and surrounded only by undependable South Vietnamese troops, I felt our life was fairly comfortable. I would not have traded it for any other job I knew about in Vietnam. I realized that the other job I might have drawn as an infantry lieutenant was that of platoon leader of an American infantry platoon. That duty would most likely have consisted of going out on three- or four-day operations, returning to two days of garrison duty in some big fort like the 25th Infantry Division, and then going back out into the jungle for another three to four days.

The other possibility was as part of the pacification effort, which would have involved leading an American platoon that would have stayed out months at a time in a small fort next to some small Vietnamese village with the mission of providing security for the people in the area. As it was, I didn't mind the operations, and living in Vietnamese villages with a mobile advisory team was not bad.

I need to emphasize, however, that, although I didn't mind the operations and actually enjoyed some of them, I always took them seriously. I was always aware that I stood one foot taller than the soldiers in our troop, and if some VC sniper decided to take a potshot from the tree line at the edge of the field, I would certainly be the target. The first time our patrol crossed a rice paddy, I tried to walk in the water and mud while the troops walked on the dikes, but after awhile I became exhausted and resigned myself to the dubious distinction of favorite target.

After several nights of lying in the sweltering heat in my bunk at night, I had the bright idea of removing the mosquito netting in an attempt to catch the breeze that floated through the bunker. I had not noticed many mosquitoes, and although everyone else slept with their nets down, I decided to roll mine up.

The first night all went well. I didn't notice any mosquitoes, and it was definitely cooler. I passed several nights like this without problems and thought to myself I should pass on the word to my compatriots that these stifling nets were not really necessary.

One night, however, while sleeping on my stomach, I awoke to a faint shuffling sound coming from the sandbag wall not far from my head. Before I could fully awaken, a rat jumped from his perch on the wall, landed on my back between my shoulder blades, ran down the full length of my body, and jumped off the end of the bed.

I immediately leapt from the bed, landing on all fours on the floor beside Skeeter, who was sleeping on the lower bunk. "What!" he shouted in a startled voice. "What's going on?"

"A rat jumped on my back!" I yelled, gasping as I peered into the darkness in the varmint's direction.

Skeeter settled back down on his bunk. "That's why we use our mosquito netting," he responded matter-of-factly. In Vietnam you couldn't take anything for granted, and you could bet that everything the experienced soldiers did had a purpose. I learned that it was necessary to protect myself from the elements as well as from the enemy. To this day I cannot stand the thought of rats.

Fortifications at Ben Cau. Most forts in Vietnam were built in the shape of a triangle because this permitted enfilade fire from the three corners. Our fort was in the shape of a square, and the main street for the village ran through the middle of it. The structure shown here is a machine gun bunker that has three firing ports.

The fort was surrounded by a fence, coils of barbed wire, and razor wire. There were numerous booby traps and land mines in the perimeter among the coils of wire. Whenever the enemy mortared the compound, which happened frequently, the machine gunner inside this bunker would fire long bursts of rounds into the tree line that was about one thousand meters away. He probably didn't know where the enemy was located but was firing in hopes of making a lucky shot.

CHAPTER 7

EIGHT VC AND A HELICOPTER

We make war that we may live in peace.

—Aristotle (384–322 BCE), *Nicomachean Ethics*

After a few weeks at Ben Cau, I went on another operation with Lieutenant Kan from the Southern village. By now Bock had left for his new assignment and Sergeant Nea had taken his place. Nea seemed very young and had a similar story to Bock's, having lost his family in a VC attack up North. He was very intelligent. He had studied English a great deal, but he was not really very conversant in English because of his limited exposure to Americans. Mack also went with us on this operation.

Our route of advance this time was to the South not far from the Cambodian border, through rice paddies and along a large area of untilled land that was overgrown with brush and bamboo. About midday, as we emerged from a patch of woods, one of the soldiers in front of me yelled, "VC!" and pointed toward a small patch of jungle on the other side of a large, open field.

Looking in that direction, I saw two men in black fatigues carrying rifles disappear into the woods. "How many?" I asked Nea. He inquired of Lt. Kan, who responded that there were eight. Pulling out my map, I surveyed the landmarks and asked Kan to point out where we were. His little brown finger rested on a spot of trail on the map. Pointing toward the small patch of jungle on the map, I said, "Then the VC are here. What will you do now?"

He looked up from the map and said, "We go this way," pointing down the trail away from where the VC had gone, in the direction of our previously designated route of march.

I was shocked that this officer, whom I had respected for his bravery on my first operation when he chose to walk point, decided to just avoid the enemy when he clearly had the advantage of superior strength and position. I believe that this incident illustrates how the attitude of the South Vietnamese people caused them to lose the war. They were brave, knowledgeable, and well equipped, but they lacked the desire to engage the enemy and fight to win.

"No," I responded, "we go this way," I said, pointing in the direction the VC had gone. I immediately called our headquarters, told them about the sighting, and said that we would begin to maneuver on the VC right away. As soon as I finished the transmission, a strange American voice came over the radio, identifying himself as the commander of an American force located in the jungle to our east, probably the area from which the VC must have come.

"I think we chased them out, and I've called for a chopper," he said. "Why don't you wait and use him to shoot up the area, over."

I said "Roger, over." Almost immediately, the voice of a chopper pilot came over the radio, announcing his arrival above us. I had Kan throw a smoke grenade on the ground to mark our position.

"I see your yellow smoke," the chopper pilot said. "Where are they?"

I gave him a direction from my compass and said, "They're in a small patch of woods only about 300 meters from our position."

"Roger, Sassy Cat Five," he said. "Do I have permission to fire?"

"Roger," I said, whereupon he fired a rocket that landed in a piece of jungle about 500 meters off target closer to where I judged the American unit was. "Gunship," I said, forgetting his call sign, "you're way off!" I gave him the direction and distance again.

An agitated voice of the American company commander (a captain, I imagined) came over the radio, saying "Sassy Cat Five, adjust from the point of impact."

"That would be difficult," I said, "because it's so far off. He just needs to try again." About that time, an unfamiliar voice came over the radio, saying that he was an FAC (Forward Air Controller) in a plane above us. He said he knew what target I was referring to and would fire a smoke grenade into the target if we wanted him to. I looked up and saw him in a very small, silver plane high above. I gave him the go-ahead, and he fired a white-colored smoke grenade directly into the small patch of woods where the VC were hiding.

This was too much for the VC, and one of our men yelled that he saw VC running from the backside of the patch of jungle. I radioed the chopper pilot to look for VC running out the backside of the wooded spot. When he replied that he saw nothing, I called him off and said we were going in. I had Lt. Kan line all of his men up on the edge of the field and march toward the tree line.

When we were about one hundred meters out, I ordered fire. Kan and his men just looked at me blankly. To make the point, I put my rifle on automatic and began spraying the trees with fire as we walked. Mack began firing. With a gleam in his eye, Nea also began shooting, and soon the whole line was firing and reloading until we reached the tree line. Of course, the VC were gone, but I felt a little better for having finally taken some decisive action.

This was the American way. When the enemy was spotted, our people would generally stop, call in firepower (helicopters or artillery), and proceed only after the area had been thoroughly shot up. I believe that this was not always the most effective method, and it taught our South Vietnamese partners a method of fighting that would be hard to sustain once we left. I considered the operation botched and blamed myself for not immediately moving against the enemy as I had planned in the beginning.

A farmer's homestead in Ben Cau. This was a typical scene in rural areas of Vietnam. The cottage is framed with timber and covered with thatch. The oxen and oxcart were essential for farming and transporting goods to market. Even the poorest people seemed to have motorcycles. They were called "Hondas" regardless of make. Even today, the sales and repair shops in Ho Chi Minh City (Saigon) are called "Honda Shops."

CHAPTER 8

THE LAST WEEKS AT BEN CAU

The Lord will guide you always;
he will satisfy your needs in a
sun-scorched land
and will strengthen your frame.

—The Holy Bible, Isaiah 58:11a (NIV)

We experienced more mortar attacks about every week. Luckily we were usually in the bunker or close enough to get back to the bunker when this happened. The event I remember most during this time was when one of our ambush patrols got into a firefight one night with a force of VC.

The fight took place on the outskirts of the village near the river about 500 meters from our fort. When it started, Captain Tail came into our bunker and requested that we call for artillery light canisters to be fired above the area to give our people a better chance to see the VC. Dai uy gave us coordinates and Capt. Smith called in the mission on our radio. When the first round came over, I stepped outside the bunker and watched the light canister slowly fall to earth on its little parachute, casting its light over the landscape below. Dai uy was in touch with his unit that was engaged in the firefight on his radio. They called back and said the light was not in the right spot. Capt. Smith told me to go out to try to determine how the light should be adjusted.

I put on my helmet and flak jacket and went out behind the headquarters building and climbed on top of the berm next to the river where I could see the firefight. The night was very dark. I could easily see the red tracers from our soldiers' rifles barking out from the edge of the village and the green tracers from the enemy's rifles streaming back from the jungle toward our people. It was difficult to determine how the illumination rounds needed to be moved, but I judged the adjustment as best I could.

I was suddenly aware that some of the enemy rounds were beginning to come my way and quickly dropped behind the berm as I heard bullets hitting the wooden headquarters building behind me. For the second time, I experienced the whizzing sound of bullets just above my head, but this time I had wasted no time getting down. Crouching as I ran, I went back to the bunker and gave Capt. Smith my estimate of how many meters in distance and the direction I estimated the artillery light canisters needed to be moved.

Once again Dai uy's patrol reported back that the light was not really where they wanted it. Capt. Smith looked at me and said in a disgusted tone of voice, "Well, I guess I'll have to do it myself." With that, he put on his own helmet and flak jacket and headed for the door.

When he was halfway out the door, I thought to give him a warning and said, "You'd better keep your head down because there are a few stray rounds coming over the berm."

Capt. Smith stopped in mid-stride with his head leaning out the door and his posterior still inside. He withdrew from the doorway, turned and looked at me with the beaded streamers still draped around his neck and said, "Really?"

"Yes, sir," I said. "Not many, but some." Capt. Smith took off his helmet and flak jacket and returned to the radio. "I'll try again," I said, as I went back outside. This time I was careful to stay low behind the berm while I made another calculation of how much the light needed to be moved. I'm not sure if we ever got the flares in the right spot, but soon the VC withdrew and the fight was over. We sent out ambush patrols every night. I would go along on some of them, and, for the most part, they were uneventful. However, there were some remarkable exceptions, which I will describe later.

Normally a mobile advisory team would stay in one location for only sixty days before being transferred to another location, but it was possible for the assignment to be extended to ninety days. One day, I believe it must have been in early July, a large metal ship came to carry our gear up river to our new home that Captain Smith said was located along highway 22 not far from Tay Ninh City. As usual, Dave organized the move. After everything was packed and organized, we were assigned several Vietnamese soldiers to help carry our gear to the boat. We discovered after awhile that some of them were carrying boxes of food and gear to their own quarters and bunkers instead of to the boat. We had Nea tell the Vietnamese first sergeant about this, and after a few minutes and a lot of shouting on the part of the first sergeant, the boxes reappeared, and we began loading the boat in earnest.

This boat was actually a large, steel landing craft with a large, metal door at the front, which was designed to be lowered to the riverbank for marine attacks. It proved to be very handy for loading and carrying our furniture and other equipment. These boats were covered with metal armor and manned with a 50-caliber machine gun mounted on each side. It was piloted from a small pilothouse topside.

After the boat was loaded, we climbed aboard for the trip up river to our new home. As I recall, Capt. Smith and Mack took the chopper into province headquarters to pick up our jeep. We would be able to use a jeep since our new duty station would be on secure roads.

After climbing aboard, I moved to the side of the boat and saw a strange sight. I saw what I thought at first to be a small, gray snake, but it turned out to be a slender lizard with tiny feet. The strange part was that it had two heads, one at each end. One head was definitely dominant and the other was smaller and undeveloped. Its feet were opposing to each other and seemed to work in opposite directions as it tried to run away. One of the Vietnamese soldiers walked up as I looked in amazement at this strange creature. When the soldier saw the two-headed lizard, he immediately stomped on it, crushing it with his combat boot. He said, "Number Ten," which was the term for "very bad" in pigeon-English. I was very disappointed because I had an idea of capturing the little critter.

The trip up the river was amazingly pleasant. The weather was good, and the movement of the boat caused a refreshing breeze to blow across us. We saw all kinds of traffic on the river, from small sampans to larger boats, carrying goods, farm produce, or animals. After about two hours on the river, we arrived at a small, well-constructed dock, unlike the dock and bridges we normally saw, which were usually rickety affairs.

The headquarters building at Tra Vo. This building was a French villa located on the edge of a rubber plantation. Regional Forces Company (RF) 766 was located here, and Mobile Advisory Team (MAT) 66 served as advisors here in August and September 1969. RF 766 was the most disciplined and best led of the RF companies that MAT 66 advised.

The company commander, who was a first lieutenant, had been severely wounded with a VC rocket propelled grenade (RPG), and never left the post, but his second in command, a second lieutenant, was highly capable and led the company on operations. Although the interior of this building was sparse, it was much better than the bunkers where the team was usually housed.

CHAPTER 9

TRA VO

The angel of death has been
abroad throughout the land; you
may almost hear the beating of
his wings.

—John Bright
Address to the House of Commons, February 23, 1855

After disembarking, we walked through a small village with the usual throng of curious villagers lining the street to observe our approach. As we drew near to our destination (a small masonry building at the end of the street) I realized that it was our good fortune to have been stationed at an old French villa that was situated in the middle of an abandoned rubber plantation. Although the building was quaint and stoutly built (twelve-inch walls), it was by no means luxurious. We had one large room for all our sleeping cots and a dining table, and a bathroom with a toilet although there was no running water. We were later shown how the toilet could be flushed with a bucket of water that was kept close by for this purpose.

In several ways, Tra Vo was much better than Ben Cau. It was located on Highway No. 22, a paved and secure road that ran between Saigon and Tay Ninh City. It was a very attractive setting with the villa set among the rubber trees. The village and the villagers seemed more prosperous than at Ben Cau, and we were not located so close to the Cambodian border where the VC were more prevalent.

We soon met our new Vietnamese counterparts and comrades with whom we would join in the struggle against the VC. Capt. Smith had come ahead in the jeep, and he introduced us to the commanding officer, who was a Vietnamese first lieutenant, Lt. An, and to his first officer, Second Lieutenant Man, both of whom seemed to be in their early thirties. I liked them both immediately.

The first lieutenant, Trung uy An, had massive scars all over his stomach, which he explained were the result of a wound from being shot in the stomach with a VC hand-held rocket launcher, called an RPG. I never questioned this explanation, but I wondered how a man could have survived being hit with such a formidable weapon.

The second officer, Tieu uy Man, was short, thin, and very competent. He kept his troops in good order and always conducted himself well. He was the one who always went out on operation with us, which suited me just fine. We also soon met our new Mama-san, who would cook and clean for us. She was a wonderful middle-aged woman, and a great cook, who treated us all like her own children. Trung uy An and his family lived in the rest of the house. The lieutenant had a habit of walking around the house not wearing a shirt, which provided us with a constant reminder of his grievous wound.

A small emergency developed the first day we were in Tra Vo, regarding our new interpreter. Nea was very young, having just graduated from interpreter language school, and though he was intelligent and knew English well, he was not accustomed to talking with Americans and had difficulty understanding at first.

Capt. Smith wanted him to relay a message to his new counterpart, Trung uy An. Nea was having trouble understanding exactly what Smith wanted to say, so the captain called for me in a very frustrated voice. "John, would you tell the lieutenant something for me. This stupid interpreter doesn't understand a word I'm saying."

Using the limited Vietnamese that I knew, along with the little English Trung uy knew, I was able to get the message across. I felt sorry for Nea. Capt. Smith never said another civil word to him.

After we had been at Tra Vo for only a couple of days, Capt. Smith was transferred to district headquarters as second in command. I was sorry to see him go. He never gave any of us any trouble and treated us well. As second in command, I took over as team leader, which suited me just fine. Although I was never particularly hungry for power and didn't plan to make the army a career, I did prefer being in charge.

The operations we conducted out of Tra Vo mostly involved working along the river. One exception was a joint operation with an American tank company. Tanks were virtually useless in our area because of the soft soil and rice paddies, but the armor officers seemed not to want to give up.

I took Dave with me on this operation, which started out to be fairly normal. We boarded Armored Personnel Carriers (APCs), which are light-armored vehicles, that moved along quite well while in the rubber plantation where the ground was firm. We rode on top of the vehicles with tanks out front and proceeded through the trees at a fairly good rate of speed. After about thirty minutes of progress, the driver of the vehicle in front of us stopped because two of the Vietnamese soldiers on his APC were fighting. The Vietnamese lieutenant in charge was called to the scene. He broke up the fight and stood the two men at attention. He then took a rifle from his first sergeant's hands and began to hit the two offenders, swinging the rifle by the barrel like a baseball bat.

After receiving a couple of blows each, the two soldiers could take no more and began running. The lieutenant chased them around for a short while, making largely ineffective swings at them with the rifle. Then they all stopped abruptly and climbed back abroad the APCs to continue the operation as though nothing had happened. When it was over, I turned to Dave with my mouth open, showing him what must have been an incredulous look on my face. He shrugged and said, "That, sir, is a Vietnamese Article 15."

In the U.S. Army, Article 15 of the Uniform Military Code says that a commanding officer may administer punishment to a subordinate for minor offenses without going through the formality of a court marshal but only with the written consent of the subordinate. I had used it several times at Fort Hood, and it served to save time and looked better on the soldier's record than a court marshal. Of course, physical punishment of this sort was never allowed in the U.S. Army.

As the operation progressed, we began to move into open areas where the ground was quite soft, and some of the tanks became mired in mud. When this happened, a large, ugly machine with a winch, called a tank recovery vehicle, was brought forward to extract the disabled tanks. The rest of the trip was a very slow and cumbersome affair. That was the only time I ever went out with tanks, and it demonstrated to me why armor was mostly useless in the southern part of the country.

As I mentioned before, most of our operations out of Tra Vo involved activities on or along the river. The first of these operations was what I call the "mouse, cheese, and cat operation." It was not billed as such, but that was what it turned out to be. We were the cheese and the VC were the mice.

The first of these operations was aborted before we even got on the boat. Dave and I traveled to the navy dock one evening with orders to join a Vietnamese platoon for the operation. The operation was canceled for reasons we never knew. On the way back to Tra Vo, Dave remarked as to his relief, thinking we had been saved from certain disaster.

"We were lucky," I said.

"No," he replied, "our mothers are praying for us."

A few days later, we were called to the naval dock again. Our orders were to board the boat with a platoon of Vietnamese soldiers and to wait for further instructions. We then proceeded to motor up and down the river in the dark (the cheese part of the operation). After a short time, the Vietnamese soldiers strung hammocks across the interior of the landing craft, giving the inside of the boat the look of an oriental Junk. Dave and I settled down on a small bench with the radio between us and began to doze in the sitting position.

Sometime around the middle of the night, the VC (the mouse) fired a rocket at us from the shore. Luckily it hit the top of the sidewall of the boat, glanced off, and exploded in the air. Pandemonium broke loose inside the boat as the soldiers rolled out of hammocks and fell all over each other. I immediately thought about how lucky we were. The rocket, which I knew must have been fired from a Russian-made RPG rocket launcher, was designed to penetrate armor siding, such as our landing craft had, spewing hot metal fragments inside as it exploded. This one had been fired too high and bounced harmlessly off the top portion of the sidewall of the boat.

I immediately called headquarters to report the incident. They acknowledged the report and said they would call in some flair canisters from the artillery in order to light up the area. Headquarters soon called back and said that the captain of the boat had been ordered to turn about and get into position so that we could launch an attack against the VC. I told Nea to inform the Vietnamese lieutenant, and we all got our weapons together and moved to the front of the boat by the large drawbridge-type door. I informed headquarters that we were going in and requested that the light flairs be continued. We had now become the cats in the game.

The engine of the boat made a terrible grinding sound as it pushed and pulled the boat around and approached the shore. The front of the boat rammed into the riverbank and the great door came crashing down. I had expected everyone to rush off the boat when the door hit the ground, but no one moved. I looked out at the silent landscape bathed in the dim light of the artillery flares. Fortunately, as we stood there as easy targets in the gaping open door of the landing craft, there was no sign of the VC.

The Vietnamese lieutenant shouted an order to disembark, but still no one moved. He moved forward, grabbing one of the men next to the door and threw him off the boat. Then he grabbed another and threw him off the boat. After a third soldier had suffered this ignoble dismount, all the others finally rushed off with Dave and me following. A search of the shoreline turned up nothing but empty foxholes, prompting the Vietnamese lieutenant to come to me, requesting advice.

As we stood on the riverbank, I looked across the field toward a tree line on the other side and reasoned that the VC had run across the field and lay in wait among the trees, planning, no doubt, to pick us off as we came across. I figured that there were probably not too many of them, maybe a squad of four of five, and decided to use the assault technique I had used before in Ben Cau. I lined everyone up on our side of the field facing the tree line, making sure there was plenty of room between soldiers. Then I gave the order to advance. At first, we all stepped out tentatively, but after a few steps, I hollered, "Fire!"

Shifting my rifle to automatic, I began firing bursts of rounds into the trees. Dave and Nea began firing, also, and so did the Vietnamese soldiers. The firing from our side was deafening, and if we received any return fire, I was not aware of it. As we got close to the tree line, we began running and swept in unopposed. We found an RPG launcher and three rockets in the trees but no enemy bodies. I assumed we must have caused some casualties among the VC or they would not have abandoned such a valuable weapon and its ammunition. It was normal for the VC to drag off their dead and wounded after such an encounter.

After reboarding the boat, we made a run up the river and then turned to head back to the naval dock at dawn. On the return trip, I went above to the pilothouse to speak to our captain. He was a young ensign who seemed very friendly, and we talked for awhile in the pilothouse on top of the boat in the cool night air.

When we arrived at the dock at dawn, we disembarked and left the rocket launcher and the three rockets with American navy personnel. Unfortunately, I heard over our radio the next day that some sailors were apparently handling the rockets when they dropped one on the dock. The rocket exploded, and three sailors were killed by the blast.

These river patrols continued at the rate of about one per week for awhile without further incident. One day I talked to the S2 officer (intelligence officer) at district headquarters, who told me that the major was also sending him out on these patrols. A sergeant first class, who was also assigned to district headquarters, had been accompanying him. This intelligence officer was a first lieutenant about my age. He told me that he actually enjoyed these patrols because he hadn't run into any trouble so far and because he could ride topside where the air was cool.

The role of an intelligence officer in such a remote location was not as glamorous as you might expect. It involved working with the local officials to try to glean information from the local populace about the whereabouts and movement of the VC. It also involved night operations into the local villages to capture or kill suspected VC or VC sympathizers. It was extremely dangerous work. I had a clearer idea of the stress imposed on these men after I returned home and met an ROTC classmate of mine who had had the job as an advisory intelligence officer. He had only served about three months in Vietnam and admitted that he had "cracked up" and had to be sent home.

A couple of weeks after talking with the young intelligence officer at district headquarters, I heard that the boat he was riding on one night was attacked with rockets and that he and the sergeant were so badly wounded they had to be evacuated to hospitals in the United States. The friendly naval ensign and several Vietnamese soldiers were killed in the same attack.

I took the death of the navy ensign particularly hard. I had only talked to him a couple of times, but one night, during an uneventful cruise up and down the river, I went topside to talk to him. It was near morning, and he suggested we stop for awhile. I agreed. He eased his boat over to the dock at Tra Vo, which was lighted with a large electric light. It was close to morning, but we sat topside, talking for about an hour. I had not had a chance to talk to another officer in a long time, and we shared information about ourselves. He was married and had a small child. We talked about what we would do when we got home and compared notes about where we had been stationed. He told me he had graduated from Annapolis.

The night that he was killed and the intelligence officer was wounded was the last of the nighttime river patrols. I figured that to that point, the river patrols had produced perhaps a couple of VC casualties that resulted from our first attack. We, on the other hand, had lost six Americans, four dead and two wounded, plus several Vietnamese. I believed that it was mostly due to carelessness on our side.

The author in light combat gear. Whenever team members left the compound, they carried, at a minimum, a rifle with ten to twelve clips of ammunition. If the operation were a serious one where contact with the enemy was expected, a steel helmet was always worn and possibly a flak jacket. Nighttime operations were the most dangerous and always prompted extra precautions and maximum equipment.

CHAPTER 10

AMBUSH, A NEW STRATEGY

Yes; quaint and curious war is!
You shoot a fellow down
You'd treat if met where any bar is,
Or help to half-a-crown.

—Thomas Hardy, "The Man He Killed" (1908)

A few weeks after the wounding of the lieutenant and the sergeant on the river, the strategy changed. I don't know if it was due to the casualties we experienced or if the people at headquarters just decided it was time for a new course of action. In any event, it was decided that we should try to disrupt VC activity along the river by using ambush patrols. The plan was to take platoons of South Vietnamese soldiers out on boats at night and drop them in predetermined locations along the river in hopes that they would catch VC patrols that were operating in the area. This type of operation, called an ambush, is a very effective use of offensive action when an army is relegated to a largely defensive role as we were in Vietnam. My first experience with these ambush patrols was less than successful and a bit embarrassing, as I look back on it. We went out with a platoon from our post with the Vietnamese Second Lieutenant Man. By this time I had great confidence in this unit and its leadership. Just after dark we loaded the platoon of about twenty men with Lt. Man, Dave, Nea, and I on a large landing craft and headed down the river.

Earlier in the day when we got the orders for this operation, Dave shook his head gravely and told me about a similar operation he had gone on in Korea. He said that his unit unloaded from a boat at night and moved inland toward a predetermined location. After only a few meters of progress inland, the first man in the patrol hit a land mine. "He was right in front of me," Dave said, "and when he hit that mine, it blew him ten feet in the air. We just gathered up what was left of him, turned around, and got back on the boat."

The vision of that story played over and over in my mind as we disembarked from the boat on a dark night and headed for the spot were we would set up our ambush. The spot was along a tree line near the river next to a rice paddy. The paddy was not flooded, but it was muddy with a couple of inches of water remaining in some places. The lieutenant positioned his men along the tree line and invited us to join him with his headquarters group on a dry spot next to the riverbank.

As we settled down, Nea remarked on the lack of cover at this location and asked what we should do in case of attack. Without giving the question the proper amount of thought, I said we should roll over the edge of the riverbank, which would give us cover. I didn't realize it in the dark, but we were actually on a small peninsula formed by a bend in the river.

Dave and I agreed that we would both stay awake all night. Nea slept on the hard ground while the lieutenant moved back and forth, checking on his troops. Sometime around the middle of the night, it seemed that the sky fell in on us as machine gun fire rumbled to our left. Bullets and tracers tore through the trees and plowed up the ground around us. Per my less than brilliant plan, Dave and I rolled over the edge of the riverbank and found ourselves in water over our heads. When I resurfaced, I saw Nea diving headfirst over me into the water. As I began to try to claw my way up the steep riverbank, which was about five feet high, Lt. Man appeared on the edge, extending his hand down to me. I grabbed it. As he pulled me out, he exclaimed, "No VC, no VC. It is boat. U.S. boat shoot at us."

As I pulled Dave and Nea out of the water, a picture formed in my mind. We were on one side of a small peninsula, and an American naval vessel with a 50-caliber machine gun was on the other side, spraying the shore with fire, which was coming through our position. We all ran toward the rice paddy for cover as the red tracers pierced the air around us and the bullets tore up the ground under our feet.

How we escaped being hit I don't know, but we all made it safely to the rice paddy. We dove behind the dike, which was only about one foot high and one foot thick, not thick enough to stop a 50-caliber bullet. A 50-caliber machine gun is the most powerful weapon in the army's arsenal of small arms. The round it takes is about five inches long, and the bullet it fires has a diameter about the size of a man's thumb. It has great penetration power and is a truly formidable weapon. As the boat rounded the peninsula, I knew we would be sitting ducks.

I tried vainly to raise someone at headquarters on my radio. There was no answer. I put out a desperate message to anyone who might hear, asking him or her to call the U.S. Navy to help us. Still no answer.

With the big machine gun still singing its deep rumbling song and bullets tearing up the ground around us, I frantically tried to think of an answer to our dilemma. I had a strobe light in my pocket, and I pulled it out, thinking I might turn on its brilliant, flashing light to signal the boat. Then a vision flashed in my mind. I imagined the machine gunner, bending over his terrible weapon, pouring fire into the shoreline. I thought, if a light flashes to his right in the rice paddy, would he cease firing, knowing a strobe must mean U.S. personnel? Or would he train his fire on the light, thinking it was a muzzle flash from someone who was firing back? It was a chance I wasn't willing to take. I put the strobe back in my pocket.

I then did the only thing I could do under the circumstances. I began digging with my hands in the soft mud below me in an attempt to create more cover from the 50 cal. bullets. I dug a hole for my head, propped my helmet up between the gun and me and submerged my head into the muddy water, holding my breath. Then I began digging a depression for my chest. Then I began praying the Lord's Prayer.

As the boat rounded the bend in front of our position, I was suddenly aware of silence. The thunderous clapping of the machine gun suddenly ceased, replaced only by the droning sound of the boat's engines. We lay very still until the boat had completely passed. Then slowly we began to stand up, brushing the grime and mud from our clothes and faces. As we stood on the little dike, I looked down in the dim light at where we had been lying. There was a depression in the mud where each man had been, but I must admit that mine was the largest and showed the most evidence of digging. Although it seemed like an eternity, the machine gun had probably been firing only about four or five minutes.

In frustration I took the radio from my back and threw it as far as I could into the rice paddy, exclaiming that it was a worthless piece of crap. Dave walked out to retrieve it. "Leave it!" I said. "It's not worth taking back."

"You'll get in trouble if we leave this out here," he said, as he pulled the radio from the mud and brushed it off. I was very frustrated with the radio because it never worked when we really needed it.

I muttered, "What are they going to do? Send me to Vietnam?"

At this point, Thieu uy remarked that we were very lucky and explained what he thought had happened. He said the enemy must have come into the other side of the peninsula beyond our vision, and not knowing we were here, fired upon the boat as it came up the river. Naturally the boat returned fire with its machine gun, and the bullets ripped through our position on the other side of the peninsula.

After some working of the knobs on the radio, Dave finally raised head-quarters and gave them a rundown on what had happened. Headquarters called the artillery and had them fire some light canisters so that we could sweep the area a bit, looking for the enemy soldiers who had fired on the boat. The sweep turned up nothing. As the sun rose, we boarded our boat again and left. Thus ended our first and most ignoble attempt at night ambush along the river.

The night ambush patrols on the river continued for the whole time we were at Tra Vo. They were conducted with varying degree of success. The VC continued to move through the area, and up and down the river was their favorite route of travel. The pattern involved the VC and NVA (North Viet-namese Army) troops moving out of their sanctuaries in Cambodia to attack our outposts and other targets around Saigon. There were other operations during the day, but they were largely uneventful.

We had two new members to join the team at this time. One was First Lieu-tenant Fred Lynch. Lynch was a nice guy from Alabama, who was what we called a "scrounger." He had considerable ability to procure supplies or just about anything else you might need at little or no expense. The other new member of the team was Sergeant First Class Crutchfield. He was in his early forties and had a full head of white hair, which was obviously why he was called Whitey. He was the most aggressive soldier I ever met. He was actually replacing Mack in order for Mack to return to the States for a thirty-day emer-gency leave. Whitey was only with us a short time, but I was glad to have him when on September 1, 1969, I received orders to report to district headquarters for instructions regarding an important operation we would conduct that night.

A few days prior to this operation, I was sitting on the veranda of our villa when some of the Vietnamese soldiers began shooting with a shotgun at pieces of broken pottery thrown into the air. After several shots, which were mostly misses, they offered me a chance to shoot. The gun was an Ithaca 12-gage pump shotgun that was very much like the one my cousin Robert used when we went quail hunting in Virginia. The gun felt very good in my hands, and warm feelings of home flowed through my mind as I broke several pieces of pottery thrown by a soldier.

Trung uy An watched from the veranda and cheered as I finished my shooting. "Number one, number one," he shouted. When I was finished shooting, I handed the gun to him. He handed it right back to me along with a bag full of shells, indicating that I should keep them. I called Nea out and asked him to explain that I could not keep the gun. The lieutenant insisted that I keep it, and added that I could return it some day before I went back to the States.

When the call came that day to go to district headquarters, I took the shotgun with me. I also took Whitey. Whitey had a very unusual weapon that I had never seen before. It was an M16 rifle with an M79 grenade launcher mounted under the barrel. This weapon is quite common today, but at that time it was a rarity.

We arrived at headquarters a little after noon. The major met us and took us to the navy boatyard. We boarded a small, open boat with a young Vietnamese lieutenant and a sailor, who worked an outboard tiller that propelled the boat. We went down river for some distance where we saw peasants working in the fields along the banks. The river was very wide at this point and all sorts of native craft were moving up and down the river as we passed.

When we reached a certain point on the east bank, the major ordered the sailor to idle the boat and stood up, pointing at the bank. Whitey spoke up in a sharp voice. "Sir, don't point! You'll tell all these gooks where we're going!"

"Right," he said. Dropping his hand and nodding his head toward the east bank, he said we would ambush tonight along the stream that ran into the river at this point. Intelligence reports had indicated that this was a major infiltration route for NVA and VC troops that were moving from west to east out of Cambodia to attack points in the central part of the country.

On the way back to naval headquarters, Whitey and I talked about how we would organize the ambush. Obviously we would put the platoon along the stream where it was expected the enemy would come. Whitey offered that we should also put one or two men on the other side of the stream to catch any enemy who might escape the ambush and try to run in that direction. This sounded a bit unconventional to me, but I took it under consideration. He was basically suggesting an "L" formation as opposed to the linear one I had in mind.

When we disembarked from the small boat at naval headquarters, the major invited us to accompany him into the office. There we consulted a large map on the wall. With the naval commander, a captain by rank, watching, the major pointed out the targeted stream and reviewed the plan for the ambush. Then he turned to me and said, "Loving, how would you organize this operation?"

In response, I picked up a red grease pencil and drew a small line along the stream that represented about fifty to sixty meters on the map. "I would concentrate our troops along here near the mouth of the stream for maximum fire power. Whitey suggests that we put one or two men on the other side, about here, to catch anyone who might try to escape that way."

The major gave me a disgusted look. With a faint sneer in the corner of his mouth he said, "That's ridiculous. You can't put anyone on that side of the stream." I was about to agree with him when he added, "And you shouldn't bunch them up like that. You should spread them out along the stream." He pointed to an area that would cover about 500 meters.

Knowing that we would only have about twenty men, including the headquarters section, I protested, "Sir, if you do that, you won't get any concentrated fire power, which is what an ambush is supposed to do. If you put those guys out there by themselves, they won't even shoot when the enemy comes by."

At that point, the navy captain stepped up to me and with an amused look on his face said, "Lieutenant, did you go to West Point?"

The question caught me off guard. I replied, "No, sir, but I know that the definition of an ambush is a sudden and violent attack with the element of surprise. We won't have any of that if our troops are spread out all over the grid square."

Still smiling, the captain said, "You sound like you went to West Point."

Then the major interrupted and asked the Vietnamese lieutenant how he would place the ambush. With a great deal of flair, the young lieutenant drew a line along the stream about 500 meters long and put a dot on the bank of the river to indicate his headquarters' unit. Smiling happily, confirmed in his position, the major looked at me and said, "Well, Lieutenant?"

"OK," I said, "We'll do it that way." I knew there was no way that this Vietnamese officer was going to spread his men out like that when we got out there in the dark.

We all went back to district headquarters, relaxed, and had some supper. While we were sitting in the dining room, I asked Nea to speak to the Vietnamese lieutenant for me. "Tell the lieutenant that when we go out tonight, it is important for all the men to stay awake."

I could tell immediately that this did not sit well with the lieutenant. Nea replied, "The lieutenant says that the men must work all day, so they must sleep at night."

"But," I protested, "if the VC come, they will kill them if they are asleep."

After a brief conversation with the lieutenant, Nea reported, "He says we must all die sometime, and who can tell when it might come?"

I answered, "Tell him it is more likely to come if we are all asleep." I could tell I was losing the battle to an ingrained philosophy of fatalism that is rampant in that part of the world and decided to forget the argument and just try to keep them awake once we got out there.

Needless to say, I didn't have much hope for this operation as we went down to the boat dock and boarded our landing craft. The major had said that the Vietnamese were supposed to send out a full platoon, which he defined as twenty men. When everyone was on the boat, I did a headcount and only came up with sixteen men, so I called the major and gave him the count. He said that he would speak to the district chief about it. After awhile, some more men arrived. We did another count that seemed to indicate we had the correct number; however, I soon discovered that some of the men were jumping off one end of the boat and coming back to be counted again in an effort to fool us.

After discerning that we had eighteen men and that was all we were likely to get, I called the major again and gave him the count. "Well, then," he said, "you don't have to go if you're afraid."

My blood boiled as I said, "We'll go anyway."

As we rode down the river, Whitey told me he had loaded a flare in the M79 tube under his M16 rifle, and if we sprang the ambush he would immediately fire it to light up the site. He also told me that he had arranged with the local firebase to fire light over our position when they saw his flair. This all sounded good to me, but I would soon relearn that the best laid plans are often changed by chance or by forces beyond our control.

The sky was overcast, and it was very dark when we reached our destination. Once we were off the boat, the Vietnamese lieutenant deployed his troops just as I expected he would, concentrating the main body over about a fifty- to sixty-meter stretch of the stream near where it ran into the river. He then put three soldiers on the bank of the river next to the headquarter section, which was comprised of himself, Nea, Whitey, and me. Whitey and I sat side by side, facing east toward the stream with the river to our backs. There were bushes along the bank between us and the river, but where the three soldiers sat, the bank was clear of vegetation.

Two hours after setting up the ambush, the Vietnamese lieutenant and Nea were both asleep. The philosophy of fatalism had taken over. Whitey and I agreed that we would stay awake all night no matter what happened. A light drizzle began to fall. The night was very still, and there was really nothing to look at.

Sometime after midnight, the eastern sky began to glow with light, and we could hear the low rumble of artillery and gunfire in the distance. I called district headquarters over the radio and asked them what was going on. The answer was that an American artillery base was under attack. We needed to be on the lookout for enemy infiltrators, individuals who might be moving through the area to either join in or return from the attack. My guess was that we would most likely encounter enemy troops coming down the stream, returning from the fight when it was over.

I leaned over and kicked Nea's boot to wake him up. I told him to wake up the lieutenant and tell him about the battle going on to the east. After hearing the news, the lieutenant got up, checked on his men along the stream, and then checked on the three security guards next to us on the riverbank. After this little flurry of activity, everyone settled down again, and I was afraid the Vietnamese would go back to sleep. It was approximately 0200 hours.

About fifteen minutes after everyone had settled down, I thought that I could hear a low bumping sound like wood hitting softly against wood. It was a soft, rhythmical sound, like thump, thump, thump. I turned toward Whitey and whispered, "Did you hear that?"

He whispered, "Yes," but gave me a quizzical shrug, indicating that he didn't know what it was. We both sat there listening for about a minute more as the sound gradually got louder. At the same time, we turned toward each other and both whispered, "A boat." I then nudged Nea and said, "A boat," while motioning toward the river.

Nea told Thieu uy, who peered around the trees at the river and reported back to Nea. Nea leaned over and whispered. "He says it is VC. What must he do?"

For a split second, I contemplated the absurdity of the question. Here we were, twenty-one men, sitting in the dark, holding what must have been about 1,000 pounds of deadly weapons and ammunition, and this lieutenant asked what should he do. I leaned over and in a low but firm voice said, "Shoot 'em!"

Thieu uy understood without translation and yelled, "Fire!" in Vietnamese. Immediately, the three men on the riverbank opened up with their M16 rifles. Whitey tried to fire his flare, but it misfired. Nea, Thieu uy, and I fired our weapons toward the boat in the river. Thieu uy only had a pistol, but I had the shotgun, and Nea fired his M16. After a few seconds, Nea tried to crawl forward to get a better shot, but I grabbed his belt and pulled him back. I didn't want him injured and not be able to use him for translation if needed.

After a considerable amount of fumbling, Whitey was able to fire the flare, and I could see a small, wooden boat, floating empty in the water. I then heard some rustling in the bushes and faintly saw movement to my front along the riverbank. I fired into the bushes where I heard the sounds and saw a shadow fall forward. The shotgun was the perfect weapon for this situation. The movement ceased, and I felt certain I had stopped a VC trying to escape the kill zone.

After a few minutes, I stopped firing, got on the radio and called headquarters to report the action and request light canisters from the artillery. While I was on the radio, I noticed that Thieu uy picked up my shotgun and fired one shot into the bushes. He couldn't figure out how to pump in another round, though, and threw it to the ground. He then wisely ran over to the stream and ordered the rest of the platoon to move over to the riverbank where the action was.

Thieu uy ordered his troops to stop firing. We all listened and watched to see if there was any sign of the enemy soldiers who had occupied the boat. The noise our weapons had been making was tremendous, and when it stopped, my ears throbbed as though they couldn't stand the silence. There was no sound or sign of them.

Suddenly I heard firing coming from the other side of the river, and I was aware that bullets were ripping through the trees to our front along the river. I sensed that the first group that we had shot in the boat was part of a larger unit on the other side of the river that had begun ferrying troops across. Our men began returning the fire, and suddenly I realized that my perfect weapon, the shotgun, was useless because it couldn't reach the other side of the river.

I got on the radio and reported that we were under heavy fire from the enemy positioned on the other side of the river and requested that artillery be fired into the enemy position. As I hung up the receiver, I looked up and noticed that Thieu uy was standing up, fully exposed to the hail of bullets that were now ripping through the trees in front of us.

I reached up, grabbed him by his belt, and pulled him down to the ground. I said to Nea, "Tell him to stay down. I don't want to lose him." The translation was not necessary, and he did not try to get up. I think he was glad that I had pulled him down so that he could stay under cover and still "save face."

After a few minutes, the light canisters appeared overhead and began to provide steady light over the area. My request for artillery was answered as the rounds began exploding on the other side of the river. I began to worry, however, that the light would now actually benefit the VC, who were still shooting at us despite the artillery rounds falling on their side. I was about to call and have the light suspended when two U.S. PT boats (Patrol Torpedo Boat) came down the river and opened up on the VC with their 50-caliber machine guns. This abruptly ended the fight. The VC stopped firing and presumably moved back into the jungle.

The navy captain, Capt. Poe, then called over the radio to inform me that he was coming to join up with us. I welcomed him and directed him to our position on the riverbank. As the two PT boats pulled up to the bank, I could see the major standing in the bow of one. By this time, our men were pulling the bodies of three VC soldiers from the water. Whitey was in there with them and came out, soaking wet, smiling, with an NVA belt and buckle that he had taken from one of the dead enemy soldiers. "I think he must have had a pistol on the belt, but I couldn't find it. Must have been an officer," he said breathlessly, the river water streaming down his face from his matted, white hair.

Our men stripped the enemy of everything but their underwear and stretched them out face up on the ground. The major was delighted and wanted to know if there were any more. We told him that we thought there might have been more and speculated that some may have escaped into the rice paddy or the surrounding foliage. I knew that I had shot one directly in front of me and asked Thieu uy to search that area. He sent two men into the bushes, but they soon returned from the thick, tangled foliage empty-handed.

The major ordered us to search the area for any who might have escaped. For the better part of an hour, we fumbled around in the dark, walking up and the down rice paddy dikes. I didn't really think that any could have escaped but figured there may be more in the water or the thick bushes that we would never find in the dark. Whitey pointed out that we were sitting ducks out there if there were any survivors. Luckily we found none. We eventually loaded every-one on the boats and headed for home.

Back at naval headquarters, the three bodies were unloaded from the boats and once again were stretched out face up on the ground. As we all stood around them, the night sky began to clear, and as if on cue, a full moon popped out, casting a pale, blue light on the bodies.

The major smiled and said, "Well, I already have three body count for this month, and it's only September 1."

I looked down at the dead man lying closest to me. His body glowed an iri-descent blue in the moonlight. As I gazed upon his rather handsome face, I was suddenly struck with the finality of death and the frailty of life. He had been alive just a couple hours before. I did not know him, and I did not hate him, but, nevertheless, we had killed him because it was our job. He would have done the same to me if he had had the chance. I thought about his shortened life. For him there would be no more warm nights like this one, no more sunny days, no family, no friends, and no unborn children. Then I thought about his soul. I looked up at the blue moon, and I wondered if he was in heaven. Was he with God? I wondered if he could see me standing there above his now-lifeless form. I wondered if God could see me standing there, unrepentant and unforgiven.

A couple of days later, we received a report over our radio that a patrol sent out to sweep the area of the ambush had found graves of two more VC bodies, which we had not been able to find in the dark. I believe one was the man I shot in the bushes with my shotgun. The major now had a body count of five, and it was only the third day of the month. This was, in my mind, the perfect operation. We killed five of the enemy without losing any of our people, and we stopped a sizable enemy force from joining the battle at the American fire-base, which was under attack when we had sprung the ambush. Captured doc-uments indicated that we were up against the VC 268 Regiment.

A few weeks later, Whitey and I received instructions to go to district head-quarters for a Vietnamese awards' ceremony. We went, and to my great sur-prise, we each were awarded a Vietnamese Gallantry Cross with Bronze Star. Capt. Poe also received a medal for firing on the rest of the enemy regiment with his 50-caliber machine gun. The Vietnamese lieutenant and his three sol-diers all received medals, also. My citation, which was crudely translated by the Vietnamese, reads as follows:

1Lt Loving John C.-SN05247347.-Hieu—Thien

Outstanding Officer, Brave and had much experience at the battlefield, was attempted in many operations to destroy the VC.

Specially in the combined operation with RF&PF Forces at Hieu Thien District on the night of 1.9.69. While exchange-fire with the VC at XT: 394.214, he always showed his calmness and bravery while closed with the Vietnamese soldiers to anti-attack vigorously causing the enemy 3 killed in action many killed and wounded were brought away, and captured 1 AK, a number of ammunition and documents.

That same day I received the Combat Infantry Badge, which is awarded to any infantry soldier who comes under fire in a combat situation. I had actually already earned it much earlier during my first week at Ben Cau during the mortar attack. Dave said that he felt that the major should have recommended Whitey and me for the Bronze Star for this action.

A few days later, Dave went to see the major. After the meeting, Dave said that he told the major that we should have also received U.S. medals, but the major was still mad because of the way I had challenged him over the conduct of the ambush. Later, the major told me that I should have disciplined Dave and should have told him to control his mouth. I never did.

The market at Ben Cau. All essential food items and many other goods could be purchased at this market. Sellers and buyers began to gather there at dawn, and by breakfast time it was pretty much over. Local delicacies included pork, live chickens and ducks, fish, squid, snakes, caged rats, and butchered dogs and cats. Fresh vegetables were also available but could be contaminated if washed in the local river water.

CHAPTER 11

A TRIP TO SAIGON AND BACK TO BEN CAU

Wars begin when you will but they do not end when you please.

—Niccolò Machiavelli
The History of Florence (1521–1525)

One day near the end of our stay at Tra Vo, Lt. Lynch came to me and said that we needed some concrete to repair the bunkers that protected the perimeter of the compound. When I replied that we should put in a requisition for some, he noted that he had already looked into that and there was none available through normal channels. He said that we needed to go to Long Bein military post and trade for some. I told him that was fine with me but that I wasn't aware that we had anything to trade. "I'm working on that," he said. "We should have some stuff in a few days."

A week later, he and Lt. An came to me with an assortment of things that had been made by some of the villagers, primarily crossbows, blow guns, fake VC flags, and red and blue scarves like the ones that some of the soldiers wore for good luck. These items, he assured me, could be traded for cement at Long Bien.

Early the next day, Lynch and I set out for Long Bien, just outside of Saigon, in a rundown truck that was almost completely devoid of breaks. Lynch drove, and he had to pump the brakes furiously for several seconds before he could stop. Considering the bad brakes and the normal, crazy traffic around Saigon, the trip was harrowing.

In Saigon the major intersections sometimes had stoplights, but most often, a policeman would be in the middle of the intersection, directing traffic. It seemed that nobody bothered to drive on the right side of the road but us. When we stopped for a red light or a traffic cop, we would look across the street at a solid line of vehicles, mostly motorcycles. When the signal was given to proceed, we would all move forward, weaving in and out among the various bicycles, motorcycles, mopeds, small trucks, buses, and the occasional car.

When we arrived at Long Bien, we went through a brief security check and entered a different world from the one I had been used to for the past five months. There were above-ground swimming pools, tennis courts, volleyball courts, dining halls, and clubs. It felt like being back in the States. I actually felt safe as we were surrounded by what seemed to be a very large and secure perimeter defense system of bunkers and barbed wire. After getting a bunk assignment, we stored our gear and rifles in lockers in our room and went out to find Lt. Lynch's friends, who, he assured me, could arrange the swap.

After checking around a bit, we ran into a tall, goofy looking lieutenant, who Lynch introduced to me as a man who worked in supply and would be able to trade for our goods. Lt. "Goofy" looked at our stuff, remarked that the VC flags didn't look very real, but said that he could probably help us anyway.

We went to his quarters, which consisted of a small room with a bed and a large polished wooden bar with four barstools in one corner. After we had each taken a seat at the bar, Goofy remarked that he couldn't believe he was messing with "a couple of dirty ground pounders from the field." "Ground Pounder" is a somewhat derisive term for infantry soldiers, and today it seems like a harmless enough remark, but at that time it rubbed me the wrong way. I felt words rising in my throat that included, "candy ass, sitting on his lazy butt while we fight the war," and I realized that I had better get out of there before I blew the deal. I also had an almost uncontrollable urge to take some slices out of that shiny wooden bar with my big knife. I was afraid that if he said anything else, the urge would be more than I could stand, so I turned without a word and went outside and kept walking down the street until I came to the PX.

At the PX, I bought a few things I needed and was about to leave when Lynch showed up. He reported that he was sorry his friend had acted so badly, but he thought we had a deal. I told him it was OK as long as we got the cement. Lynch said that he was going out that night with Lt. "Goofy" and his buddies and invited me to come along. I declined.

That night, after freshening up a bit, I walked down to the Officers Club for some dinner. It was a rather pleasant place, comfortable but not elaborate. The room was full of long, wooden tables and chairs. I settled in at a table next to a major and a captain and ordered a drink. Two Vietnamese bar girls immediately sat down and began talking to me. It was obvious they had already worked the other officers with no luck and were concentrating on me. We had been warned not to divulge a lot of information to bar girls because they might be tempted to sell it to the enemy.

The girl closest to me introduced herself as Jenny and asked for my name. "My name is Nguyen," I said, knowing that Nguyen is the most common name for Vietnamese men.

"Nguyen? I never heard of GI named Nguyen," was her reply.

"That's strange," I said, "I've never heard of a Vietnamese girl named Jenny." After a few minutes they left when they realized that I was not going to buy the Saigon tea, which was watered down tea at very expensive prices that GIs bought to keep the girls at their table.

I ate a good steak dinner and spent the rest of the evening talking and drinking with the other two officers. At about 1200 hours, I left the club and began walking back towards my quarters to get some sleep. On the way back, I had to walk down a long street flanked on each side with wooden clapboard buildings. The street ended near the perimeter of the base where I needed to turn right for a short walk down another street to my quarters.

As I approached the intersection of the two streets at the perimeter, a red car pulled up under a street light on the other side of the barbed wire fence. A man wearing a light-colored shirt and dark pants jumped out of the car, shouldered a rifle, and to my amazement began firing at me. I instinctively jumped behind the building to my left as I heard bullets rip through its wooden siding. The ground was hard and dusty, and I hit it hard as I dove behind the building.

After a few more shots, the car and rifleman roared off down the street. Almost immediately a jeep pulled up beside me with four heavily armed GIs on board. As I stood up and brushed the dust off my pants, a sergeant jumped from the jeep and said, "Sir, you shouldn't be here. Somebody was shooting up on the perimeter a moment ago."

"I know," I said. "They were shooting at me!"

The sergeant said, "Right, sir." He jumped back into the jeep and drove it up to the fence, but, of course, it was too late since the VC were long gone.

As I completed the walk back to my quarters, I wondered how many men had been shot at while here in this very secure place. Very few, I reasoned. Lt. "Goofy" had probably never, and would never, ever hear a shot fired in anger. I had been there for only one night, and had become the target of some VC Saigon cowboy. I didn't feel fatalistic about it, but I did wonder how long I could continue to have these close calls and not be hit.

The next morning at 0600, Lt. Lynch and I met a supply sergeant, who loaded a whole pallet of bagged cement on our truck. We left for home. I don't remember the trip back to Tra Vo, so it must have been uneventful. We pulled into our compound sometime around midday to see everyone running toward the north side of the perimeter. We followed and found several soldiers standing around a man who was sitting on the ground with his right foot blown away from mid-calf down.

The Vietnamese medic arrived the same time we did and applied a tourniquet and bandage. I looked into the wounded man's face and was shocked to see a blank expression. He never spoke or cried out or even whimpered. He looked straight ahead with a blank expression on his face. It was a stoic look I had seen before and would see again on the faces of the hurt and wounded. Even the Vietnamese children never cried. In their culture, it was not condoned.

Soon after the trip to get the supplies, Lt. Lynch was sent home to the States. He had severe migraine headaches that would occasionally drive him to blindness. I knew he would have to leave when he had a severe attack while he and I were out on a night operation with a Vietnamese platoon. He became blinded by the migraine, and I had to lead him back by the hand. I have often thought about how silly we must have looked—two grown men, walking hand in hand through the jungle in the middle of the night, carrying M16 rifles and wearing full combat gear. I went with him to Saigon the next week to sign the papers to send him home. After he had been gone about a month, I received a letter from him. Needless to say, he was happy to go back to his wife in Arkansas.

By the end of September we received orders to return to Ben Cau. Before we left Tra Vo, Trung uy An arranged a party for us. It was a bittersweet affair. We were all treated as guests of honor at a lavish dinner in Trung uy's quarters. Each man in my team was given a special gift. I received a yellow and red braided shoulder band and a picture that was painted on a wooden panel. The background of the picture was black. The subject was a pair of small birds and a small bamboo plant painted in bright yellow and gold. I was given a postcard with the painting that read:

DEAR LIEUTENANT LOVING
WE SEND YOU A GIFT FOR MAKING A MEMORY
IN THE DAYS WITH US FIGHT VC AT "TRAVO POST."
ALL OF R.F. 3.766 COMPANY WISH YOU GOOD LUCK.

I had grown fond of the people, officers, and men at Tra Vo and hated to leave. On the day of our departure, I brought out the shotgun and gave it back to Trung uy. He handed it back to me and said, "You keep. Kill many VC." I accepted it back and promised to return the gun before I went back to America. Mama-san cried, and there were many misty eyes and farewell salutes as we walked down the company street to the river where the boat loaded with our gear awaited. I must say that the unit at Tra Vo was the only really competent Vietnamese combat unit I served with in Vietnam.

Once again we boarded the large boat and headed up the river northwest toward the Cambodian border. When we arrived at Ben Cau, we unloaded our gear and moved back into the large sandbag bunker. It was as though we had never left. Captain Tail and his lieutenants were still there, and I recognized many of the soldiers from before. They all made a big deal of our return. Tail could have been offended to have me, an officer of lesser rank, assigned as his counterpart, but he showed no sign of it and accepted me warmly.

The local officials also recognized our return. I was visited by two of the three village chiefs. The chief of the northernmost village showed up one day, driving a rickety old jeep. He said he wanted to take me on a tour and show me the sights around his village. I agreed and, shouldering my shotgun, climbed abroad next to him in his jeep. The chief spoke passable English so it was not necessary to take Nea. We crossed the bridge and drove around his village for about thirty minutes. I wondered if there were any VC watching and they were, as I would learn later.

Nevertheless, the tour was without incident, and we ultimately stopped at the chief's house. It was a modest abode made of unpainted clapboards with a rusty, tin roof. He took me inside where I met his wife and daughter. His wife smiled pleasantly and his daughter, who was a small, pretty girl, looked down at the floor respectfully. According to Vietnamese custom, they both immediately left the room. The chief and I sat on his floor for a few minutes and drank a brand of beer called 33, a Vietnamese brand that you can still buy in Vietnamese restaurants in this country. In those days, this beer was preserved with formaldehyde, which gave it a distinctive taste. It was not cold because the chief had no electricity.

After finishing the beer, he drove me back to our fort, and on the way back, the chief asked me if I had a wife. I replied, "Yes," and told him about my wife in America.

He asked, "But do you have a Vietnam wife?" I was perplexed by the question. I said that I did not have a Vietnamese wife. He smiled broadly and said, "Then you must have my daughter for your Vietnam wife."

I was so astonished that I could not answer for a moment. I tried to think what to say. I had only met this man today and he was offering his daughter to me as some short-term wife. She was a very attractive girl, but I instinctively knew this would be trouble. "But," I protested, "in a few months, I will go home to the United States and would have to leave your daughter here alone."

"No matter," the chief said, "after about one year, you come back. She wait."

I did not know how to respond. "No, *co debt qua* (the girl is very beautiful), but I must have only one wife, and I will not come back." He seemed very disappointed, but, nevertheless, he gave me a warm farewell when he returned me to our fort.

This incident brought home a couple of points to me. Many of the Vietnamese officers and officials assumed that we would be there forever, providing them with support and protection from the VC. They did not understand that I was part of what was called "Vietnamization," which was a policy designed to turn the country over to them and prepare them to defend themselves. They were assuming that we would always be there. They thought it was good to give their daughters to us because it would further bind us to them. Americans had been there a long time, and it was reasonable to assume that we would be there for a long time to come.

Some American soldiers had similar attitudes. They had Vietnamese girlfriends and even children, and they extended their tours, returning year after year as soon and as often as they could. The Vietnamese families liked it because they received cigarettes and other goodies from the PX. One time in the PX, I saw a sergeant I knew, buying a gas-powered refrigerator. When I asked him what he planned to do with it, he said that it was for his girlfriend's mother. When American forces withdrew from the country, we left thousands of Amerasian children behind who were ostracized by the Vietnamese people then and still are today.

The chief of the middle hamlet also came to visit. He invited himself in and had a seat at our table. He was a small, thin man who did not speak as much English as the other chief. I offered him a cold beer that he readily accepted. I got one for myself and sat down to talk. The conversation was limited because neither of us new enough of the other's language to say more that a few perfunctory remarks.

He downed his beer quickly and asked for another after burping loudly. I got him another, which he also drank quickly while burping as much as possible. After three or four beers, he seemed a little drunk, so on the next round, I gave him a Sprite. He drank that quickly, too, once again finishing with a loud burp.

Dave muttered, "That gook is going to drink up all our beer." I sensed that the chief considered himself to be out drinking with the boys, so I decided it was time to call a halt to the party. I got up from the table, shook his hand, and said that this had been fun, but it was now time for him to leave. As he staggered out the door, he said that I must come to his house tomorrow for dinner.

The next morning Nea informed me that I was, in fact, expected at the chief's house for dinner at noon. I got directions and walked down the street, arriving at his house on time. The chief was very formal, greeting me at the door and bowing low. I returned the bow and entered his home with a smile on my face. His home was modest. The doorway was low, and I had to lean over to enter. The floor was dirt, but there was a small rug in the middle of the room. A small, low table had been placed in the middle of the rug. There were two plates on the table, two small teacups, chopsticks, and a large spoon. The chief sat down on the floor behind one of the plates and invited me to do the same behind the other. Soon his wife appeared with food and hot tea, which she poured into the small cups.

In Vietnam it was not customary for women to eat with the men. The women served and the men ate. It was polite to ask the woman to join the men, but she never would. After the chief's wife served us, I said, "*Cam on Ba*," meaning, thank you, madam. She obviously was very pleased and smiled as she served. When she returned to the kitchen, I said in Vietnamese, "Madam, please join us." She didn't answer, giggling without leaving the kitchen.

The meal was good, but there was very little conversation since I spoke little Vietnamese and the chief spoke little English. We drank some 33 beer, whereupon the chief again went through his burping routine. After the beer was drunk, I rose and stepped to the door of the kitchen and thanked the chief's wife again. She only giggled. Then I thanked the chief, bowing low. I left. I had done my diplomatic duty with two of the three chiefs, and, frankly, was not very concerned about the third. I didn't know it then, but I was to meet him later under very strained circumstances.

The nightly pinochle game. Entertainment in the rural areas of Vietnam was very limited. The Team had a television, but shows consisted mostly of reruns. *Star Trek* and *Bonanza* were the favorites of most GIs. The only recognizable thing on the radio was the U.S. Armed Forces channel, which did play current pop music. News was limited to only what the military wanted the troops to hear, and there was a marked lack of objective reporting. Soldiers heard less about the overall picture of what was happening in Vietnam than when they were in the States because of the lack of objective reporting.

CHAPTER 12

THE VC AND THE SNAKE

For what can war, but endless
war still breed?

—John Milton
On the Lord General Fairfax at the Siege of Colchester (1648)

Our second stay at Ben Cau was a full sixty days and the most eventful period of my tour. We began operating immediately, and I went on most of the operations. The first one was quite memorable, occurring on a clear and pleasant day early in October. It was a two company-sized operation and the group commander, Captain Tail, and I went with the southern company that was commanded by Lt. Kan, the older Vietnamese lieutenant who accompanied me on my very first operation. Under our rotation system, it was Mack's turn to go with me.

We went south into an area of jungle mixed with fields of tall grass. As we crossed one of these fields, long, slender, green snakes, five to six feet in length, moved through the grass ahead of us. Since snake meat is considered to be quite a delicacy in that part of the world, some of the Vietnamese soldiers began to chase them, trying to club them with their rifle buts. Their efforts to catch these snakes were largely unsuccessful, and often comical; the men would chase after the snakes, until suddenly the snakes would turn in mid flight and began to chase the soldiers around the field. When one soldier began shooting at a snake, Capt. Tail called an end to the snake hunt, and we began moving ahead into an area called the Hobo Woods. I believe the area got its name because it was a hideout for VC who were infiltrating from Cambodia into South Vietnam. It had been defoliated with Agent Orange and bombed several times, but the jungle was starting to grow back. It was riddled with underground tunnels and bunkers.

As we approached a particularly suspicious-looking bunker, Lt. Kan drew his 38-caliber pistol from its holster and cautiously approached the open mouth of the bunker. After a few steps, he paused briefly to adjust the wire-rimmed glasses on his nose and moved closer, peering into the dark entrance to the bunker.

Suddenly I heard the bark of two gunshots, which seemed almost simultaneous. The lieutenant had fired at a VC crouching in the mouth of the bunker, and at the same time the VC had fired back. The VC missed the lieutenant, but the lieutenant's bullet went though the VC's hand, smashing the grip of his pistol and entering his chest. The VC was wearing a white shirt and dark pants. He looked more like a businessman than a soldier. He died immediately with a bullet in his heart. We decided the VC was a high-ranking Communist official because of his civilian dress and the documents he was carrying. His pistol was a U.S. issue 45-caliber auto loader, which must have been captured in a previous engagement. The enemy considered this weapon to be quite a prize, further evidence of the likely high status of this dead VC.

As we moved through and out of the woods, a group of our soldiers emerged with a huge python snake draped over their shoulders. The snake was still alive but had been rendered harmless by having his tail tied in a loop with a piece of twine and his mouth pinned shut with two large safety pins. They placed him around my shoulders and Mack took my picture. Unfortunately I have lost that picture. I suspect it was one that my son Matt liked to keep in his room along with a picture of me at the ceremony when I received the Vietnamese Gallantry Cross. In addition to the python, the men also had two of the long, green snakes that they carried home for supper.

That night I got a lot of satisfaction from telling the story of Lt. Kan's killing of the VC in my after-action report to headquarters over the radio. It must have sounded something like an old western showdown in Dodge City. I remember the radio operator at headquarters saying something like, "Are you kidding?" when I finished the account. After giving the report, I went outside just as the men were skinning the python. Hanging from the rafter of the head-quarters building, the snake appeared to be about nine feet long. Later they cut him up into steaks and fried them in a pan over a charcoal fire. I tried some, and it was delicious, reminding me of the taste of fried frog legs I had eaten as a boy on my uncle's farm in Virginia.

That night the Vietnamese medic shot himself through the foot with his 45-caliber pistol. He said he was cleaning it. His bunker was very close to ours, and when we heard the shot, I immediately ran over to investigate. The bullet went through the top of the arch of his foot and out the bottom. It was a very clean wound, and Skipper cleaned it and bandaged it.

It was one of those wounds that didn't bleed very much. Sometimes that would happen, but I really didn't understand why. With these types of wounds, it seemed that the flesh would pucker up and hold the blood. At other times, a more minor wound would bleed a lot. The medic was in a lot of pain, but I couldn't get him out by helicopter because it was night, and he wasn't in danger of losing the foot.

It was about 1600 hours when it happened. I checked on him at 2000 hours and found him lying on his bunk in a lot of pain. I went back to our bunker and went to bed but woke up about midnight and couldn't get back to sleep. I grabbed my flashlight, slipped on my boots, and went back to check on him. He was sleeping soundly despite the pain. We dusted him off by medical helicopter at dawn the next morning.

The author. This picture was taken inside the bunker at Ben Cau where there was very little light. This bunker, which was made of sandbag walls with large timber supports and a tin roof, served as sleeping quarters, dining room, kitchen, and work station. The refrigerator was powered with bottled gas, and a gasoline generator provided light for a few hours at night before bedtime.

CHAPTER 13

ATROCITIES

*What difference does it make to
the dead, the orphans and the
homeless, whether the mad
destruction is wrought under the
name of totalitarianism or the
holy name of liberty or
democracy?*

—Mahatma Gandhi
Nonviolence in Peace and War (1942)

Soon after arriving back in Ben Cau, I received orders to investigate an incident involving the killing of a Vietnamese civilian by an American soldier. It was the second time I had received such an order. The first time was while we were still at Tra Vo. It was a day when I was sitting on my bunk inside the villa, cleaning my equipment. A Vietnamese soldier came running into the room and told me in a very excited voice that we needed a medical dust-off for a woman who was injured out on the highway. I went immediately to the radio and called in the dust-off. Then I grabbed a smoke grenade and asked the soldier to take me to the injured woman.

Highway No. 22, the major road between Saigon and Tay Ninh City, ran right past the gate to our compound. The traffic was very heavy on this road and I assumed that a car or a truck had struck a pedestrian. When we reached the scene, I saw a small, older woman lying face up on the side of the road. The right side of her head was bloody and she appeared to be unconscious. "What happened?" I asked. The soldier who accompanied me spoke a fair amount of English and tried to explain what had happened.

"Helicopter came down from sky and hit woman," he explained. A very improbable image flashed through my mind of a helicopter, swooping down from the sky, smacking the old woman in the head, and returning to the sky. The woman appeared to be less than five feet tall, and it was hard for me to believe a helicopter had struck her. I questioned the soldier, who questioned other people who had witnessed the incident.

As more information came in, I did begin to believe, and the picture became clear. This spot on the highway was a bus stop where people congregated to catch the bus to Tay Ninh City. A U.S. chopper came flying down the road, traveling south away from Tay Ninh toward Go Dau Ha. The pilot was flying low and buzzing the people along the road for sport. When he got close to the bus stop, he dropped down to just a few feet off the highway. Everyone except the woman heard him coming and dove to get out of the way. The woman was apparently hard of hearing and didn't jump. One of the skids of the chopper smacked her head, knocking her to the ground.

As I heard this story, I looked at the woman. She was not moving and appeared to be dead. She was about my mother's age, I thought. She was someone's mother, maybe a grandmother, and some asshole has probably killed her for no reason. As I thought about this, I was overcome with sadness. How could we ever hope to win the hearts and minds of these people if our men were doing things like this to civilians?

Soon the dust-off chopper was on the scene above, and I threw out the smoke, which was purple in color. I was so distracted by my thoughts that I threw the grenade up-wind. The smoke engulfed me like a fire. I breathed in the smoke and began coughing violently. The chopper came in, picked up the woman, and headed for the hospital. When I arrived back at the villa, the pilot came over the radio and said the medic on board wanted to know the cause of the injury.

"She was hit in the head by a chopper skid," I reported.

There was a long pause on the other end, and then the response was, "Really?"

"Roger," I said. "Some asshole dropped down out of the sky, smacked her in the side of the head, and took off."

Another long pause. "Roger."

I didn't know what happened to her, but I assumed that she died at the hospital. The next week, I was asked by headquarters to write a report, which I did. It was almost impossible to determine which of the many choppers in the air at the time did this hateful deed. I doubt that the pilot was ever found out, but I have always hoped that he was made to pay for this atrocity in some fashion.

It may be apparent by now that I had a love-hate relationship with helicopter pilots. I saw them at their very best and their very worst. They were no different than the rest of the combatants in Vietnam. Most pilots were wonderful young men who performed heroic deeds almost every day. A few were scoundrels, but there were also many fearless ones who were honorable and risked their lives to bring firepower to the battlefield to help soldiers like myself on the ground. They were often the angels of mercy, risking their lives to save others who were wounded and dying and needed to be evacuated to the hospital. The day would come when I would desperately need both, and they would not disappoint me.

At Ben Cau I was asked to investigate the death of a Vietnamese boy who was killed by an American officer. He had lived in the lower village, and Dai uy Tail volunteered to take me there to meet the boy's father. We traveled on motorcycles. Dai uy and I each rode on the back of Hondas at a charge of twenty-five cents each. We arrived there quickly and went directly to the home of the father. He was a farmer who lived on the edge of the village. His home was a small wooden shack with a grass roof and a dirt floor. Like many other farmers, he lived in the village but would go out each day to work in the fields. He was a small, thin man, stooped at the shoulders from years of hard work in the rice paddies. His skin was dark and wrinkled from being in the sun all of his life. He was probably only in his late forties or early fifties, but he looked much older

Dai uy introduced me to the man, who bowed low and invited us into his house. There was very little furniture in the house. All I saw was a small table, some low sleeping platforms, and an oil-cooking stove. The man gave me a low stool to sit on while he and Dai uy sat on their haunches in the Vietnamese style. I was amazed how this grieving father, having just lost his son, greeted me with respect and with no apparent anger or animosity. I had dreaded this meeting because I assumed that the father would take out his grief on me. I thought he would be resentful and angry toward me, but he was not. He seemed to be able to separate me from the American who had murdered his son.

As the father talked, Dai uy translated. He spoke very slowly, as though the words were painful, but he seemed determined to relate the events that surrounded the death of his son as witnesses had described them to him. As the man spoke, a picture of his son's death took shape in my mind.

The boy had risen before dawn as was his custom, as was the custom for most of the village people. He had a brief breakfast with his mother and father and then prepared to go out for the day to watch over the small herd of cattle that belonged to the family. His mother handed him a handkerchief, containing two, small rice cakes that would be his lunch. He put the corners of the handkerchief together and slid them under the rope belt that held up his baggy black pants, forming a little pouch by his side. He wore a faded, brown T-shirt with three small holes in it that had been washed many times. As he left the cottage, he retrieved a slender bamboo rod from the side of the doorway that he used to prod the cattle in the direction he wanted them to go. He was four-teen-years old but small for his age.

As he stepped outside, he noticed that the sun was just barely rising above the treetops at the edge of the village. He went to the small pen next to the cot-tage and drove out the three animals, consisting of two large water buffalo and one milk cow. It was a routine they all knew well because it was what they did each day at this time of the year. At other times of the year, the rice paddies would be in cultivation, and buffalo would be working in the paddies. But now the days consisted mostly of trying to find enough grass in the fields to fill their stomachs. These were mostly quiet, lazy days, and the boy and his charges all walked slowly down the trail past other houses to the edge of the village and out into the fields.

By the time the boy reached the field, the sun was bright and the day was already getting warm. He tried to find shade as the cattle moved about the field, sniping blades of grass. He stood first under one tree and then under another. Sometimes he squatted on his haunches under a tree. Other times he stood or squatted in the open in the hot sun. At times he had to go out and tap one of the animals with the slender bamboo rod and turn it back into the proper field.

On the way out to the field, the boy had noticed a large bevy of helicopters pass over. He knew from past experience that this meant that the American soldiers would be looking for VC in the areas west of the village. He knew it was important to stay away from the soldiers, but it should be no trouble this day since they seemed to be landing far west of his location.

This war was a puzzle to him. He had seen the VC come and go, and sometimes he would hear them late at night as they passed close to his cottage. The war waged around his village at times, but for the most part, the villagers were not part of it. He had no idea what they fought about. The lives of his family members were what they had always been, hard days eking out a poor living from the ground. It did not matter to them who ruled in Saigon or who was running the country. Their lives were the same regardless, the same as it had always been for them and their ancestors going back a thousand years.

About mid-morning, his attention had lapsed. Looking up from a shady spot under a tree, he noticed that his animals had strayed across the field and needed to be turned back. He rose and started walking briskly across the field to retrieve them. When he was about halfway across, he noticed a small helicopter, circling high above the field. He stopped and looked up at it curiously. It began to descend rapidly. As he watched in amazement, it settled down on the ground in front of him. It was much smaller than the others that had flown over earlier, and it only held two men.

One of the men opened the door to the helicopter, stepped out, and rapidly walked over to him. The boy smiled at the man. He had only seen Americans up close a few times before, and they had never been a threat. The man was very tall and had very white skin like he had not been in the sun very much. He wore a clean, pressed, green uniform. He spoke to the boy, but the boy did not understand him.

The man seemed to be getting angry. He was asking for something, but the boy could not understand what. The boy said, "*Khong biet*," meaning, "I do not understand." Finally the man produced a small card, pointing to it and the boy understood that the American wanted the boy to show him some identification, but he had none. He was merely a boy, the son of a poor farmer. He had no need for such things, so he only shrugged. Again he said, "*Khong biet.*"

The American became very angry and struck him, knocking him to the ground. Then the man reached over and grabbed the handkerchief from his belt, pulling it loose. The two rice cakes rolled out onto the ground. The man then walked back to the helicopter and flew away. The boy was frightened but relieved that the man had left. His first thought was to run home to his mother, but then he remembered the cattle. He would have to retrieve the cattle. By now they were well across the field, straying into someone else's territory where they would not be welcomed. He jumped to his feet and ran after them.

After only a few minutes, he had them rounded up and was driving them back across the field toward home. Then he saw the helicopter again. It was the same one with the same two men, and it descended quickly, falling toward him. He forgot about the cattle and began to run toward the village. As he ran, he heard a loud explosion behind him. Looking over his shoulder as he ran, he saw the same man, leaning out the window of the helicopter. The man threw a hand grenade at him. This grenade exploded closer than the first but still did not hit him.

The boy ran faster and weaved back and forth across the field as the man continued to throw grenades at him, fortunately missing. There were other people at the edge of the field but they did not help, could not help. Finally, after several misses, one of the grenades fell close enough that several pieces of shrapnel hit the boy in the back and legs. The blast pushed him through the air and knocked him to the ground. He rolled over and looked back at his attacker. The chopper had landed, and the man was getting out with a rifle in his hands. Despite the pain and shock of his wounds, the boy rose to his feet and began to run again. The last thing he was heard to say before the man shot him was, "Mama."

I was so moved by the story that I couldn't speak. At first I was over-whelmed with anger, and then I was overwhelmed with great sadness. I knew that the war was full of such stories and that they were being played out all over the country. They had been replayed many times over the years. There were tragedies like this on both sides. There were also American boys being need-lessly wasted, and most likely, the last thing they thought of was their mothers.

When he was finished with his story, the old man looked down at the dirt floor. I saw the top of his head. His hair was mostly gray and very thin. I felt extremely sorry for him. I thought he would probably like to cry, but his cul-ture would not let him cry. I felt like crying myself, but my pride would not let me. I stood up. Dai uy also stood up and flashed me a nervous smile. I said, "Tell the father that I will write a report and try to make the man who did this answer for his action."

After Dai uy translated, I shook hands with the man and said, "*Toi xin loi,*" which means "I am very sorry." I was glad that I could at least offer this brief apology in his own tongue. He bowed low and smiled, seeming to appreciate the effort. Dai uy and I bowed and left.

After leaving the father's home we visited with two other farmers who had witnessed the killing. I wrote down their testimonies and thanked them for the information. Then Dai uy and I returned to our headquarters in the middle hamlet.

That night back in our bunker, I wrote out my report. I had made careful notes about the date and time of the incident, and I was careful to include these in the report. I also included the two eyewitness reports. I noted that the perpetrator of this crime was obviously a senior officer who was overseeing a large offensive operation on that day at that hour in that location. He was riding in the passenger seat of an LOH (light observation helicopter), which pegged him as a senior officer, probably a major or colonel. Anyone with access to the records should have been able to figure it out. I also made an inquiry of the American firebase in our area and discovered that there was a unit operating in the vicinity of the crime out of that base on that day. I hand-delivered my report to district headquarters the next day.

Several weeks passed and I heard nothing although I asked occasionally over the radio. One day after an operation, I was walking up the dusty road from the southern village, heading back to our bunker in the middle hamlet, when I passed the pay officer from headquarters. He was a finance captain, and each month he would come into our camp by helicopter with our pay in little envelopes. He would pass them out, take up money from any men who wanted to buy government bonds, and then take off to the next outpost. This day he was out in the hot sun, sweating profusely as he walked down the road. When we met in the middle of the road, I stopped and said, "Hello, Captain, what are you doing way out here."

His answer was, "I'm going to the next village to pay off an old man whose boy was killed."

"How much is a boy worth these days," I asked with much sarcasm in my voice.

He answered the question matter-of-factly as though it was not unusual. "Two hundred and fifty dollars." That was certainly a lot of money for a poor farmer, but I suspect some justice would have done more to win over the people of Ben Cau.

I never found out if the officer who committed this atrocity was punished in any way or not. I hope that the payoff meant that he was, but most likely, the incident was swept under the carpet. I believe that the real cause of this tragedy was the relentless pursuit for body count that was still prevalent in 1969 even though the stated goal was pacification and Vietnamization. It was obvious that we had not won many hearts and minds in the southern village in the fall of 1969. It clearly demonstrated to me why we were losing the larger struggle even though we were winning most of the battles.

Atrocities occur on both sides in every war. In this regard, Vietnam was probably no better or no worse than any of the other wars that American boys have fought. Although the two instances I have described both involved officers (a helicopter pilot, who was probably either a lieutenant or a warrant officer, and a commander, who may have been a major or a colonel), it is most often enlisted men who are involved in these atrocities.

In every situation, it is always the officers who must control and direct the actions of their men. These things are less likely to happen if the men know that their immediate superiors will not tolerate them. The rule goes all the way up the chain of command. When there is a breakdown in leadership, then we have horrific incidents like My Lai with Lt. William Calley in Vietnam and national embarrassments like Abu Ghraib in Iraq.

As conflicts drag on year after year as they did in Vietnam, the likelihood of atrocities grows. It is a difficult challenge for the officer leaders. We must encourage our men to do an unnatural, uncivilized thing—to kill. And yet try to keep them civilized at the same time. Our men must be both ruthless in their pursuit of the enemy and compassionate toward the innocent. It is a difficult, but essential, challenge. If the men are not controlled in this regard, some will invariably commit unspeakable acts. Some people will say it is because of rage or frustration over the loss of comrades, but this is not a justification, and it must never be tolerated, particularly where noncombatants are concerned.

In addition to being a moral outrage that should not be tolerated, atrocities committed by our troops also have deleterious effect on the outcome of our efforts in the occupied country. An army in the midst of an invasion, such as the invasion of Iraq, can suffer a few instances of improper behavior on the part of its combatants and not experience any long-term consequences (other than the obvious moral and, hopefully, legal consequences for those committing the crimes). However, when an army becomes an ally of the "host country," a euphemistic phrase for the occupied country, then the atrocities can and do have a long-lasting and detrimental effect on the war, or occupation, effort.

Consider the old man in Ben Cau who lost his son. He was a gentle man and apparently took his $250 and went on with his life despite the loss of his son. Suppose, however, that he had been more resentful, as he had every right to be. Suppose he had bought an AK47 with the money and had joined the resistance. Who would blame him? In fact, if you were his neighbor or his relative, would you not consider joining him?

We can easily take one damaged individual and multiply him into five or ten more recruits for the resistance. Sometimes well-meaning actions that are directed at the enemy go astray and cause the deaths or wounding of innocents. These events also can serve to recruit or engender sympathy for the enemy. These mishaps are a normal consequence of war and, though they are often avoidable, they are more understandable.

These expected mishaps will undoubtedly grow the insurgency. When you add to them the intentional acts of atrocities, the problem can grow from a small element of dissidents to a large and formidable force united by what is considered a righteous cause. As this account continues, there will be more opportunity for us to explore this concept of the "righteous cause" as it existed in Vietnam and will always exist when a foreign military presence is introduced into a country.

Two South Vietnamese Soldiers at Ben Cau. The South Vietnamese soldiers were often an enigma to Americans. At times they would expose themselves to great danger by standing up during a firefight or taking other unnecessary risks in order to "save face." At other times they would purposely avoid contact with the enemy when they had obvious advantages of superior numbers and firepower. As with all armies, the performance of these troops varied considerably, based upon the competence of their leaders. The good-looking young man on the right was seriously wounded when his rocket launcher exploded.

CHAPTER 14

NIGHT AMBUSHES AND VC IN THE VILLAGE

The day is done, and the darkness
Falls from the wings of Night,
As a feather is wafted downward
From an eagle in his flight.

—Henry W. Longfellow, *The Day Is Done* (1845)

After we had been back at Ben Cau about three weeks, I received a call from district headquarters to report with one of my men for a three-day trip to a neighboring village in the southernmost part of the province. Apparently the major had volunteered us to accompany a local Vietnamese company on night ambushes in the area. They had successfully sprung an ambush two days before, killing two VC, and the major thought they might repeat the event if we were along.

That afternoon, Mack, Nea, and I climbed aboard a helicopter to take a short ride south to the small village, which was located southwest of Go Dau Ha. When we disembarked at the village, we were led to an American captain, who had also been sent there to conduct joint operations with the Vietnamese.

He then introduced me to a young Vietnamese lieutenant in charge of the local Regional Forces. He had set up his headquarters in a rather large, wooden building in the middle of the village.

The captain explained that one of his American lieutenants would take out one of his platoons while I would go with a Vietnamese platoon to ambush outside the village that night. It seemed like a pretty simple plan. We would all hike out into the middle of a large rice paddy nearby, and as the sun went down, we would split up with the Americans going into the woods to the left and our Vietnamese platoon going into the woods to the right. The idea was to arrive at our respective locations just after dark so we could set up our ambushes without being observed by any VC or their spies.

We knew that enemy spies were prevalent, but we would soon learn that they were more active than I had previously imagined. The Vietnamese Communists have now disclosed that their spies were everywhere. They were seemingly common people—children, women, and old men—who paced off distances to our facilities and to important targets within our facilities and gave detailed reports to the enemy. We are now told that Vietnamese barbers were favorite recruits because they learned all kinds of useful information while cutting the hair of the men and officers inside U.S. bases.

Since we had a couple of hours before we had to go out, I sat down on a bunk to rest for awhile. After only a few minutes, two young Vietnamese soldiers came in and stood before me, one of them repeating a word that sounded like the Vietnamese word for medicine. I shook my head and said I did not understand.

After a few minutes of not communicating in this fashion, the young man dropped his shorts, revealing that his private parts were terribly infected with venereal disease (VD). I stood up, told the two men to stay where they were, and went outside to find Nea. I told Nea to find the Vietnamese commander and to bring him to me. When they arrived, I told the lieutenant, with Nea translating, that his man was terribly sick with VD and that he must be sent to the hospital in Tay Ninh as soon as possible. The lieutenant agreed and they all left, considerably shortening my rest time before the operation. I never understood why the man came to me first instead of to his commander, unless he thought he wouldn't be treated without my intervention.

At about one hour before dusk, I met up with my Vietnamese counterpart and the American lieutenant. I reviewed the operation with them, looking at the map and marking the route and ambush positions with my grease pencil. As we started down the road through the village with our patrols, the American lieutenant walked by my side. He was short and a bit heavy. "Did they tell you about me?" he asked.

"No," I replied anxiously.

"Well," he said, "this is my first operation."

"You must mean this is your first ambush." I said cautiously.

"No," he said, "this is my first operation. In fact, this is my first day in the field."

"Don't worry," I said. "You'll be OK. Just follow me."

He smiled, looking relieved, and we proceeded on down the road.

Just as we came to the edge of the village, enemy mortar rounds began to fall on our position. We all crouched down at the side of the road, and I observed that we had immediately taken a couple of casualties among the Vietnamese civilians. It was a very uncomfortable feeling to be in the open with little cover to get behind. It was merely a matter of chance whether a round would fall near us or not.

Soon the Vietnamese lieutenant was at my side with coordinates of where he thought the VC were located. I tried to call in an artillery strike on the target on my radio but got no response. The Vietnamese lieutenant grabbed my arm and led me across the road to a small fort where he had a radio set up with a tall antenna. The operator found our frequency, and I was able to call in the fire mission. Soon our artillery was falling in the nearby woods, and the enemy fire ceased. The spies had not only informed the enemy of our time of departure, they also had pinpointed the very moment that we would be approaching the edge of the village. It was not an encouraging introduction to the new American lieutenant on his first day on the job.

When the firing had ceased, we all got up and proceeded to move out again. When we reached the middle of the rice paddy, it was almost dark. I nodded toward the tree line on the left, showing the American lieutenant where he was to take his patrol, and told him we would meet him back at the same spot in the morning. The rice paddy was large, and by the time we hiked across it to the right wood line it was dark.

The Vietnamese lieutenant picked a spot he liked next to a well-traveled path and had his men dig foxholes and set up their claymore mines. He had his men dig foxholes for Mack and me as well as for himself. The ground was soft, and the work went quickly. Before long, we were all settled down in our foxholes with our weapons pointing down the trail.

Soon, a gentle rain began to fall. At first it was a refreshing relief from the heat, but after awhile, the rain became steadier and became quite unpleasant. I was tired, and despite the rain, I fell asleep in the middle of the night. When I awoke, it was raining hard, the night was pitch-black, and I couldn't see two feet in front of me. My foxhole had filled with water up to my waist. It was one of the few times I remember being cold in Vietnam.

I rose out of my foxhole, sat on the edge, and leaned over to talk to Mack. "Hey, Mack," I whispered. "You OK?"

"Wet," he said.

"I know, pretty miserable," I said. "Can you tell what time it is?"

"No, can't see a thing," was his reply.

I told Mack that I would tell the Thieu uy that we should leave right before dawn so that we would get back to the middle of the field by first light. I told Nea, who then told the lieutenant, who agreed, and we all hunkered down for what seemed to be another couple of hours.

Finally, the sky began to lighten a little, and we all got up, secured our weapons, and retrieved the claymore mines. It was still fairly dark as we left the woods, but by the time we began weaving our way across the rice paddy dikes toward our rendezvous point, it began to lighten. The rain slackened and was replaced with fog. As we came closer to the middle of the field, I began to see what looked like large, black humps sitting on the dike in the middle. At first they reminded me of a heard of black cows, lying in a field in the rain, but as we drew closer, I realized they were the American patrol. I figured they must have left their position even earlier than we did to beat us back to the middle of the rice paddy.

As I approached the lieutenant, I said, "You must have left really early to get back here before us."

"We never left," he replied. "The men thought they saw some movement in the trees and refused to go any further."

I looked around at these men, and they were the most pitiful looking American soldiers I had ever seen. Of course, they were wet and dirty, but most of all, they were just beat down. There was a look of deep fatigue and despondency about them. There was no spark of life, and they reminded me of large lumps of wet, green moss sitting there in the fog.

That day, and many days since, I have asked myself what I would have done if I had been that young lieutenant, facing a platoon of rebellious soldiers. I decided that I would have taken my senior NCO and would have scouted out the ambush site. Then I would have returned to tell my men that it was clear and that we were going in. I would have said that any man who didn't go with me would be court marshaled and that if any man ever refused to obey my order again, he would find himself in the stockade in the morning. I hope I would have done that. I cannot really say, though, because, thankfully, I was never in that position.

I didn't know it at the time, but that morning I had witnessed a new, rebellious attitude that was developing among some U.S. Army units in 1969. This attitude was akin to a sickness that would spread through a unit and eventually overtake the entire enlisted personnel. In some rare instances this illness would result in a despicable practice called "fragging." This would occur when the men would attack their officers, particularly using fragmentation grenades. *Vietnam, a Chronicle of the War*, with text by Michael MacLear, declared, "Prior to 1969 'fragging' was apparently so rare that official statistics do not record any incidents. Between 1969 and 1971 assaults on officers in Vietnam averaged 240 a year, eleven percent fatal." I hope that this unit never reached that level of rebellion, but they were definitely headed in a disturbing direction.

What I saw that day was merely a symptom of a larger problem that was overtaking the army in a general way. As the peace talks in Paris dragged on, our soldiers were reduced to fighting for a nebulous cause, which was to hold on with no clear goals or objectives until it was over. Prior to Tet of 1968, our army fought to win. After Nixon took over, the goal was to negotiate a settlement and gradually reduce the number of U.S. troops in country. The effort took almost another four years, and the slow, grinding pace, accompanied by continuing significant casualties, began to erode the moral of the military.

The army began to see rising instances of fragging, desertion, and outright rebellion among the troops. Speaking further of this sickness, MacLear states, "It is hard to escape the conclusion that Commander in Chief Richard Nixon, through his doubling of the war years without military objective, left a once proud army morally shattered. The American public would finally judge Nixon for his administration's political degeneracy; the demoralization of the military was probably no less dangerous."

So it was that from sometime in late 1968, our men were expected to soldier-on without a clear objective or mission to win. For the great majority, they continued to fight valiantly for duty and honor, which is a large part of what soldiers have always fought for. However, we now know that duty and honor is a dish that is best served up along with a main course of support and gratitude from the nation.

During the day, the American company pulled out and I have no idea what happened to the young second lieutenant and the rebellious platoon. On the walk back to the village, he had asked me what he should have done. I told him, and I hope it helped him.

That night, Mack, Nea, and I went out on another ambush with the same Vietnamese patrol. This time we were told to ambush in the middle of another large rice paddy. We set up on a large mound in the middle of the paddy. It was raining when we left, and I was prepared for another miserable night. The rain was relentless, and I sat with my rifle between my legs, my arms folded over my knees, and just let the water pour over me, becoming soaked to the skin.

Sometime around 0200 hours, the rains began to let up, and Nea stretched out on the ground to try and get some sleep. As the rain subsided, I smelled a foul odor. Suddenly Nea sat up and began to wipe his clothes with his hands. "What is it?" I asked.

"Shit! Shit everywhere!"

"Is it buffalo shit?" I asked.

"No!" he exclaimed, "people. People shit."

I jumped up, suddenly realizing that the little mound we were sitting on was basically an outdoor latrine, which had probably been used by Vietnamese farmers for hundreds of years. The thought was disgusting. I told Mack to be careful about where he sat and then told Nea to tell the Vietnamese lieutenant we were going back early and to pack up his people. As we walked back, the rain started up again, and I was thankful for its cleansing effect.

When we got back to the village, it was about 0500 hours. All of the Vietnamese soldiers stopped at a small cafe brightly lit with lanterns and full of farmers having breakfast before they went out to the fields. I passed it up and went to the well I knew was located in the middle of the village.

I poured a bucket of water over my body and scrubbed myself as best I could. Then I went back to the café and sat down at a table with the Vietnamese lieutenant, Nea, and Mack. It was very pleasant, sitting in a dry place among friends, and I ordered a cup of French coffee and a French pastry. The coffee and the pastry tasted so good that I felt I had never had better. When the sun finally came up, we all headed back to headquarters, got soap and towels, and returned to the well for a good scrubbing. That afternoon we were ordered back to Ben Cau, and we were happy to go "home."

Back at Ben Cau we continued to operate normally with two of our men going out each day on operations with Vietnamese platoons. We were regularly mortared every other day or so, and there were small actions during this period, but nothing I remember much about except one night when I woke up to the sound of a Vietnamese voice, shouting over a loud speaker.

Captain Tail came over to our bunker and explained that the VC had entered the upper village and were shouting propaganda messages over a portable loudspeaker or megaphone. "What will you do?" I asked.

"Nothing," he said. "Nothing to do."

I asked Nea what the VC was saying. Nea listened intently for about a minute and answered, "He is saying the people should kill the Americans."

I looked at Dai uy Tail and asked him again what he was going to do. After some thought, he went back to his bunker and retrieved a map. Spreading the map out on our table, he showed us where he had two small ambush patrols set up on the outskirts of the village. Then he explained how he could try to move them in to attack the VC who were broadcasting from the middle of the village.

That's more like it, I thought, and quickly agreed to the plan. Dai uy began to maneuver the two patrols over his radio to put them into position where they could attack the VC. After a few minutes, I became aware that the broadcast had ceased, and I began to worry that the VC would get away. After a little more time, there was a brief burst of gunfire and then more silence. Dai uy began yelling frantically into the radio mike, trying to raise his men to find out what had happened.

After several very long minutes, there was finally a response on the radio. I saw a frown come across Dai uy's face. He put the mike down, looked up at me, and said, "They shoot each other. Two of our men dead."

I was shocked. "I'm sorry," I said. Tail did not answer. He just stood up, shook his head sadly from side to side and walked back to his bunker. "I'm sorry," I said again.

I knew it was my fault. This was death from friendly fire, which was a polite way of saying you screwed up and killed your own men. I had pushed the situation when Captain Tail knew it was not wise. Their deaths fell on my shoulders and still rests there today. It is the thing I regret most about my service in Vietnam.

Cobra AH-1 Gunship. This helicopter carried a crew of two, pilot and copilot, and was used solely as a gunship. Armed with both rockets and machine guns, it was a very formidable weapon. As advisors, the members of MAT 66 were responsible for calling upon and then directing fire from these aircraft.

CHAPTER 15

THE CAMBODIAN INCURSION

It is well that war is so terrible.
We should grow too fond of it.

—Robert E. Lee, the battle of Fredericksburg, December 13, 1862

One afternoon, Dai uy Tail came to me and said that he would like for us to go into province headquarters in the morning to meet with his Vietnamese S3, Major Trang, who was the man he replaced in Ben Cau, and with our U.S. S3, Major Barton, to discuss a proposed operation. In the morning we flew together on the supply chopper to headquarters.

We went to Major Trang's office at which time Major Barton joined us. After exchanging salutes and handshakes, we all sat down around a large map of the province that was spread out on a table. The Vietnamese S3, who spoke a fair amount of English, pointed to a spot just inside the Cambodian border and said that the VC had set up a base camp there. He wanted Dai uy to take elements of two companies into this area and burn the structures that had been built there by the VC. He expected that the VC would run, but if not, we should kill as many as possible.

The plan seemed simple, and I agreed to the strategy. Major Barton said that he and Major Trang would monitor the operation from a helicopter circling above. I wondered if the Cambodian government knew we were going into their country and suspected that they did not. I decided not to ask because I figured it was not my problem, and it wouldn't change anything. I was in favor of going after the VC wherever they were if it would make our sector more secure.

The day before the operation, we got our orders by code over the radio. When I plotted our route of travel, I saw that it showed us being dropped next to the border by helicopters, but it did not show us going across. I told Mack that I wanted him to go with me. He reminded me that it wasn't his turn, but I told him that this was a special operation and that I needed him. He nodded his head, indicating that he understood, and accepted the assignment without complaint. I began to realize that I depended on Mack quite a bit. He was young and strong, and he had a considerable amount of valuable experience.

The next morning, October 22, we got up and had our breakfast as usual. Mack got up from the table and went out into the courtyard. He immediately came back with a very worried look on his face. "This is going to be a terrible operation," he said. "The Vietnamese soldiers are armed to the hilt, and their women are standing around crying and telling them good-bye like they are not coming back."

I grabbed my gear and went outside to find the situation just as Mack had described. I had never seen our troops so well prepared before. They had machine guns and LAWs, and they were all wearing boots and helmets. Mack came back out wearing a flak jacket, which was quite a statement on what was bound to be a very warm and humid day.

The day started badly. As we all stood around in the courtyard, preparing and adjusting our gear, one of the Vietnamese soldiers I knew was standing next to me. He was carrying a LAW, which is an antitank weapon that looks like a collapsible tube. When opened and extended, it becomes armed. It has adjustable sights and is fired by pushing a button. It is disposable, and once fired, you merely throw away the tube. It fires a very powerful rocket that is capable of penetrating armor or fortified positions. It is a light and very portable alternative to carrying a recoilless rifle (bazooka).

The soldier removed the LAW from his shoulder and sat it down on the base of a concrete monument that was in front of him. As the LAW touched the concrete, it unexpectedly fired, making a loud noise and pulverizing his face. He was only about six feet from where I was standing. Miraculously I was not hit, only slightly stunned by the explosion. I immediately went to him, kneeled down, and examined his wounds. I don't know if he was hit with pieces of the rocket or pieces of cement, or both. His face was a mess, but he was still alive.

I ran to the radio inside our bunker and called for a dust-off helicopter, while his compatriots bandaged his wounds as best they could. The chopper got there really fast, and a few minutes after it departed, the medic on board called back to say that the man would probably live but was sure to lose both eyes. Prior to this accident, the young man was probably the most handsome man in the entire Ben Cau force. I never saw him again.

After we got the injured man out, we all walked into a nearby field and loaded into choppers for the short flight out to the border. It was the largest airlift in which I had ever participated. There were several choppers, carrying about eighty men in three lifts. Dai uy Tail, Mack, and I rode in the same chopper. As we landed, I immediately heard the sounds of battle.

We were coming into a hot landing zone (LZ). There was a small compound of six or seven wooden buildings to the west just across the border, and our men were receiving small-arms fire from it. I saw two VC soldiers come out of their compound and begin to fire a machine gun at our people. Soon, mortar rounds began to fall randomly in the field where we were spread out. I watched through binoculars as our people moved to the left and attacked the nearest building. They took the building quickly, and soon it was burning from their torches.

Major Barton came over the radio and said that he and Major Trang, the Vietnamese S3, were on station above. I gave him a report on what was happening below and said I would keep him advised. The mortar rounds began to fall fairly regularly, and I estimated that the enemy must have been firing two or possibly three tubes at us.

As we moved closer to the action, the VC small-arms and machine-gun fire also began to come our way. We were standing in the open with no cover to get behind, and it became very uncomfortable as bullet rounds began to kick up the dirt around us. We were between 300 and 400 meters from the VC machine gun, but, fortunately for us, the Vietnamese on both sides were notoriously bad shots. Most of the rounds fell short or wide of our position. After only a short time, there was another building smoking as our people put a torch to it.

A few minutes after the second building began to burn, two of our men were brought to us with serious wounds. Both had head and neck wounds and needed immediate attention. One had a large bandage over his forehead and eyes, indicating possible eye and face damage. I immediately called for a medical chopper to evacuate the wounded. Mortar rounds continued to fall around us, some very close, and the VCs on the machine gun continued to fire at our people who were nearest to the village.

After only a few minutes, the pilot of the medevac came over the radio and asked me to throw smoke to mark our position. Dai uy was standing next to me, and I asked him to have one of his people throw smoke. Instead of throwing the smoke grenade, he handed it to me and backed away. I pulled the ring and threw out the grenade, which was red smoke.

It was standard procedure to throw the grenade and then ask the chopper pilot to identify the color. The VC would sometimes listen in on our frequency, and when they heard us say we were throwing smoke, they would also throw out a smoke grenade, trying to lure the chopper to their position so they could shoot it down. This had been dramatically demonstrated to me a week or so earlier. At that time, I received a request from Dai uy to call for a medevac for one of his patrols that had a wounded man in the field about two kilometers west of Ben Cau.

When the chopper came on station, I had Dai uy tell his men to throw smoke. The pilot identified the smoke as yellow, but when I asked Dai uy what color his men had thrown, he said that it was purple. I quickly alerted the pilot not to go to the yellow smoke. Eventually the pilot spotted the correct smoke and safely landed to pick up the wounded man. I called for an artillery strike on the location of the yellow smoke, but I only managed to wound an innocent farmer in the field. The VCs who threw the yellow smoke probably escaped.

The farmer had a nasty gash on his upper arm, and I watched as the Vietnamese medic sewed it up with about ten stitches. The man stood motionless through the ordeal and never even grimaced. When it was done I went to him, bowed, and said, "*Toi xin loi Ong*," meaning, "I am sorry, mister." He bowed in return and smiled at me very warmly. I was amazed at the forgiveness shown by this humble man and wondered it I could be so understanding if the tables were turned.

On this day when we were standing next to the Cambodian border, the smoke grenade that Captain Tail had handed me proved to be red when I threw it. The chopper pilot identified the smoke correctly and said that he was coming in. I suddenly realized that Tail and his men were running away from us as the VC concentrated their fire on the helicopter and on the red smoke grenade I had just thrown. In addition to the mortars, the enemy small arms and the machine gun began to also rake our position with fire. As the chopper came into our position, it kicked up a lot of dust that mixed with the smoke and debris from the mortar rounds that were impacting on our position. The combination of dust, smoke, and noise from the chopper and the mortars created a frightening scene that caused all of the Vietnamese soldiers around us to scatter.

Mack and my radio operator helped the two wounded soldiers onto the chopper as mortar rounds fell dangerously close. There was no cover because we were standing in an open field. I reported the situation to Maj. Barton over the radio, and he informed me that he had already called for gunship helicopters, which were on station above us. I asked Mack to give me a distance and direction to the machine gun. Despite the numerous bullet rounds and mortar explosions impacting around us, he pulled out his compass and map and made the calculations.

In a very short time, the gunship pilot came over the radio. "This is Red Dog above you. What can we do?"

Before departing, Dai uy had given me coordinates of where his men thought the VC mortar crews were located. Mack gave me his estimate of the direction and distance to the machine gun. "Red Dog," I said, "this is Sassy Cat Six. I want you to shoot up the following targets."

I gave him the coordinates. After a short pause, Red Dog came back over the radio. "Sorry, Sassy Cat. No can do. That target is in Cambodia."

I was astonished at the response. "Do you mean to tell me that they sent us in here and did not give you permission to shoot into Cambodia?"

The answer was, "That's a roger, Sassy Cat. Sorry."

At about this time I was vaguely aware that someone was calling my name in a very loud and agitated voice. I looked up to see Mack standing a few feet away, yelling at the top of his voice, telling me that our Vietnamese counterparts had completely left the field. We were facing the enemy alone. I looked at my radio operator, who now had a look of terror on his face, as deafening explosions erupted all around us.

My first inclination was to run and catch up with the others because I had a vision of being captured, which I thought would be worse than being killed. But instead of running, I decided to stay. I resolved that I would not leave until we had finished our mission and inflicted whatever damage we could on the enemy. He had come to our village many times and mortared us, killing or wounding soldiers and civilians alike. He had come into our village at night, intimidated our people, and exhorted them to kill us in our sleep. He had moved with impunity across this border to attack, assassinate, and terrorize on our side, and then he had been able to return to safety across this imaginary line, merely a black line drawn on a map. Now he was doing it again, and our troops did not have the gumption to confront him. I had had enough. We were finally in his backyard, and I didn't want to leave until we had done him some damage.

"Mack," I yelled, trying to carry my voice above the din of the exploding mortar rounds, "I will not leave until I have called a fire mission on these bastards. Will you stay with me?" He considered the question for just a moment and then the look on his face turned from one of concern to one of resolve. "I'll stay," he said as a mortar round landed behind him shaking the ground where we stood.

I then turned my attention back to the gunship circling above us. I had to yell into the radio mike in order to be heard above the roar of the exploding mortar rounds. "Red Dog," I yelled, "this is Sassy Cat Six," emphasizing the "six," meaning the caller was a commander. He didn't know that I was only a first lieutenant. "I'm the commander of this operation, and I'm telling you that this is Vietnam, not Cambodia. I want you to shoot up that target and anything else you see that looks like the bad guys."

It was a very improbable assertion since everyone knew it was not Vietnam, but I realized that I couldn't order him to shoot into Cambodia. In fact, there was probably no one in the whole province who could order him to shoot into Cambodia, so the only thing I could do was to advocate for it being Vietnam.

After a long pause, "Roger," was the response. "This is Red Dog, and I am attacking this target based on your order, and I note that your call sign is Sassy Cat Six."

Almost immediately, the chopper unleashed a horrendous volume of firepower from rockets onto the machine gun emplacement on the other side of the border. It was completely knocked out. The enemy compound was totally unfortified since the enemy had never before needed to worry about being attacked in their sanctuary.

At about this time, Maj. Barton came over the radio and asked me to relay a message to Dai uy Tail. I responded that I couldn't relay a message because Dai uy wasn't there. "You should never be separated from your counterpart," he said.

I didn't know how to respond. I didn't want to tell him that Tail ran off while Mack and I were taking care of his wounded men. I said, "During that last mortar barrage, it was necessary for us to go in separate directions."

After a pause, Maj. Barton answered, "OK, just tell him to call his S3 when you catch up with him."

I then gave Red Dog the suspected coordinates of the VC mortar crew. After a couple of passes and more rocket fire from the chopper, there was a secondary explosion, leading me to think we had knocked out at least one of the mortars. Red Dog came over the radio, saying, "I have people on the ground, running. Shall I fire?"

"What direction are they running in?" I asked.

"West," was the answer.

I figured that they were the rest of the VC who had been with the machine gun. I said, "Roger, Red Dog. Go ahead." Another burst of fire erupted from the ship, but I couldn't tell the result.

At about this time, Mack insisted that we pull out before it was too late. Because I had been absorbed with the fire missions over the radio, I hadn't noticed that our RF troops were now completely on the other side of the large field, almost out of sight. While I had been working the gunship over the radio, Mack and my radio operator had been standing there watching the mortar rounds fall, knowing that at any moment the next one might fall on us. Mack had stood firm when the others had run. He had carried the wounded to the helicopter and had lifted them aboard while we had been under intense fire. He had risked his life to do his duty, and, although I didn't know it at the time, he would do it again before the day was done. Now, he wisely knew that it was time for us to get out while we still could.

We began to run as fast as we could to catch up to the RF soldiers. When we reached the other side of the field, we found Captain Tail and his troops resting under a border of small trees. There were two more very seriously wounded soldiers there, and once again I called for a dust-off. As the chopper came into view, Tail pleaded, "No more smoke. Use this." He held up the backside of his map, which made a nice white panel.

I picked up the radio mike and said, "Dust-off, we cannot throw smoke because it draws fire."

"Never mind," he said, "I see your panel." Whereupon he dropped down to about fifteen feet off the ground and came directly toward us. The enemy apparently saw him also and began lobbing mortars at him, which fell around us as well.

Dai uy and his troops scattered again, leaving Mac and me to load their two wounded soldiers. Mortar rounds fell around the chopper and us. Mack carried one man and I carried the other to the chopper. As we helped them aboard, one round of mortar landed directly on the other side of the chopper. I heard the distinct sound of metal hitting against metal as the shrapnel dug into the body of the aircraft. How we escaped being hit, I do not know.

Once the helicopter had lifted off the ground, I got back on the radio. "Red Dog," I said, "This is Sassy Cat Six. I need some more ordnance." I gave him the general vicinity of where I thought the fire was coming from. By now Red Dog was happy to shoot anywhere we wanted, assuming the blame would fall on me if there were any repercussions. Shortly, the incoming mortar rounds slackened, and Mack and I had to once again run in order to catch up with our troops. They had had enough of this mini Cambodian invasion and were heading for home.

I didn't know if Dai uy had received permission from his commander to withdraw or not. I wanted to stay and fight some more, but there was no way I was going to stay by myself, and it was more than obvious that he had no intention of staying. I never knew how many of the enemy there were, but I suspected there were quite a few, including enough mortar crews to keep rounds pouring down on us constantly.

By the time the last mortar round fell, it was almost 1200 hours and we had been in combat all morning. Captain Tail estimated that the enemy had fired approximately 120 rounds of mortar at us over the course of the morning.

We were about five or six kilometers from home, and we walked back, having lost our opportunity to bring in another airlift. After covering about half of the distance, we came to a small river, which had to be crossed. The river was only about twenty feet wide, and a single narrow board had been laid across it as a bridge. All of the Vietnamese, including Dai uy, nimbly walked across like tightrope walkers as the board swayed back and forth.

After much contemplation, I decided to try it since the only alternative was to swim. I decided to run across, hoping that speed would propel me to the other side. I was about three-quarters of the distance across when I fell off the board.

On the way down, I hit my right knee on the board, the same knee I had injured playing football in high school and re-injured on the obstacle course at Fort Benning. The water was over my head. I swam to shore, but first I had to hold onto my rifle and helmet so as not to lose them. Some of the men helped me climb out of the steep bank. Standing on the shore, I must have looked like a drowned rat while the Vietnamese were still dry and neat looking. After watching my ignoble plunge into the water, Mack found a shallower spot some distance up river and waded across with water up to his chest. My knee hurt for several days after that, but there was nothing to do for it.

About a week after the Cambodian incursion, Dai uy came to me saying that he had good news. The Cambodian police had investigated the area of the battle and reported that our helicopter fire had killed eleven VC. Later intelligence reports estimated the total enemy losses of killed and wounded enemy at twenty. Everybody at province headquarters was very pleased, and Maj. Barton recommended Mack for the Bronze Star with "V" and me for the Silver Star.

Our district major was not pleased because he felt that I should have maneuvered our men against the VC positions. I didn't feel that I could tell him our Vietnamese soldiers ran off and could not be maneuvered, so all I said was, "The only thing I could do was direct gunship fire on them." He was not satisfied and told province headquarters that he did not support the medals. I think his real beef was that he was not consulted or involved in the operation. I received another Gallantry Cross with Bonze Star from the Vietnamese for this action but never received the U.S. Silver Star. Maj. Barton was killed during the real Cambodian invasion a few months later, and I suspect that the award died with him.

Mack and I each wrote accounts of the battle that we sent up to headquarters. While the majors argued over territorial issues, I signed the paperwork recommending Mack for the Bronze Star with "V" for valor. When I saw his proposed citation, I was surprised to note that it stated that our RF troops had "scattered," since I had been careful not to mention this in my eyewitness report. That information must have come from Maj. Barton. I left Vietnam not knowing whether Mack ever received his medal, but I knew that he deserved it.

None of us in Tay Ninh Province knew it at the time, but a full-scale invasion of Cambodia would begin in April 1970, which was authorized by President Nixon. I have always wondered if our little attack across the border had been some sort of test case. It had proved that the enemy was very vulnerable there. Their facilities were not fortified, making them susceptible to our superior firepower. If our Vietnamese troops had advanced instead of retreating, I feel certain that we could have produced many more casualties among the enemy, possibly wiping out their entire force in that location.

Water Buffalo. These beasts of burden are actually a species of caribou and were used extensively in the rice-growing regions for pulling plows in the rice paddies. When not being used for work, they were allowed to graze in the fields, usually under the watchful eye of one of the farmer's children. They had a natural hatred of Americans and were likely to charge if not deterred by their diminutive masters. The animal on the left has dropped its head in preparation for the charge but was prevented from doing so by the little girl with her switch.

CHAPTER 16

THE U.S. ARMY COMES TO TOWN

There's many a boy here today who looks on war
as all glory, but, boys, it is all hell.

—Gen. William T. Sherman, Columbus Ohio, August 11, 1880

As November began, we continued to go out on daytime operations and send out night ambushes. The most significant thing I remember was that one day, some soldiers in our camp caught two little boys outside our bunker with a hand grenade. The boys were apprehended, and when questioned admitted that they were planning to throw the grenade into our bunker. They named an older man in the village as the person who had put them up to it. The man was arrested and sent back to province headquarters for interrogation.

I had heard other stories about the VC using children to attack GIs, but I never expected it to happen to us. We had always let the children come and go freely without giving it much thought. After that, the guards of our fort were more careful about whom they let into our area. This incident illustrated how much the VC objected to our presence at Ben Cau and how they tried to use our acceptance of the children against us. It also indicated that the VC were painfully aware of the progress we were making and had decided to single out our team for elimination.

Early in November, a U.S. Army rifle company showed up at Ben Cau and set up camp outside the southern hamlet. The company commander, a tall, red-headed captain came to our bunker and announced that they had been assigned to stay with us awhile and help the locals defend themselves from the VC. I don't remember his name but I'll call him Captain "Red." He was a very tough, no-nonsense officer, educated at the Citadel. He set up two, 81mm mortars in the company street in front of our bunker and made our place his headquarters. He enjoyed cooking on our stove, watching some television with us in the evenings, and occasionally playing pinochle. With Lt. Lynch gone, it was nice having another officer around.

About the third day he was there, Capt. "Red" announced that he could supply materials, cement, and sandbags to build a fort in the southern village. The Vietnamese would need to supply some laborers to work with his men. Dai uy arranged a meeting with the chief of the southern village to discuss the matter. This was the one chief who had not come to call when I took over the team.

The meeting was held in Dai uy's bunker. Capt. "Red" described his plan, with Dai uy translating for the chief. The village chief was rather large for a Vietnamese, and I suspected that he might have been part Chinese. He was an older man with white hair. He listened intently and then answered that the plan was good but that the Americans would have to provide some money to pay the laborers who would help dig the moat and create the berm around the fort. Capt. "Red" seemed irritated by this request. He said that he had no money to pay the people. The chief then turned to me and asked if I could provide a little money to pay the people. I said that I did not have any funds at my disposal, which was a true statement. Capt. "Red" argued that he was supplying the materials and men and expertise and that the Vietnamese could at least provide some labor. The chief shook his head, indicating he did not know what to do.

At this point, I also became a little irritated with the chief, thinking that this was the least they could do. I said to the chief, "Someday we will have to go home. I will no longer be here, and the Americans will not be here to protect you. And then the VC will come. If you are not strong, they will come into the village, and the first thing they do is kill the chief." I looked squarely at the chief as I said this.

He knew it was true. It was such a simple truth, but it was like it had not occurred to him before. He said, "OK." He would find the people somehow. On the appointed day of the construction, there must have been one hundred laborers there, men and women, young and old, digging the moat and packing the earth into a berm. It was finished in one day.

When we went out on operations with the Vietnamese platoons, "Red" would also send out one of his platoons in a flanking pattern. One of his NCOs would come along with us to coordinate with his comrades over the radio. I remember going on one of these operations when the Vietnamese lieutenant and this American NCO got into a disagreement over where we were standing according to our maps. To settle the dispute, the NCO called for an artillery smoke round to be exploded above where he thought we were. The round exploded some distance away, proving our Vietnamese officer to be correct. The incident made me realize that I had a great advantage of never having to worry about being lost when I was with the Vietnamese soldiers, despite their other shortcomings.

At about this time, our area seemed to be the subject of several experiments with unconventional means of warfare. For awhile, we were assigned two very large German shepherd dogs with their handlers. The dogs could not stand the heat, and I could not see where they served any useful purpose. Then we were assigned two snipers, who spent each night sitting on the berm to our compound, looking through their starlight scopes at the surrounding countryside. If they spotted any likely targets, they would ask permission from Dai uy to shoot. He never granted it, thinking the targets they picked were just villagers outside going to the bathroom in the middle of the night.

One night a small helicopter was sent out to pick up Capt. Tail and me to ride with an American forward observer. The idea was that if we saw anything suspicious, we would authorize the forward observer to call in artillery or air strikes. Of course it was pitch-black out, and we didn't see anything suspicious until I looked down and saw green tracer rounds climbing toward us. Someone on the ground was firing a heavy-caliber gun at us. Fortunately, the pilot used evasive action, banking sharply to the left and removing us from danger. We gladly authorized a strike on the area from which the tracer rounds came and then called it a night and returned home.

One day the supply chopper brought in two young fellows along with a strange contraption, which was described as a type of ground radar. I was told that this was the pet project of a general. I was to provide whatever assistance the operators needed and to notify headquarters if they had any trouble. The radar was dubbed the "rabbit" because of its two, large antennae that looked like TV rabbit ears. The idea was that this contraption would be able to track enemy movement out in the field at night. The two operators picked a spot on the berm and set up their operation.

The first night I went out and inquired how the "rabbit" was working.

"It doesn't work," was the reply. "It never has and it never will. But we don't mind sitting out here with it because it beats humping in the paddies." I went back to the bunker and forgot about it.

One evening several days later, I was watching TV in the bunker with Capt. "Red" when one of his men was carried in with numerous grenade fragments in both legs. When "Red" inquired as to what had happened, the man explained that at about sundown a water buffalo charged his position. "My buddy threw a frag at it," he said, "and I dove to get out of the way, but the shrapnel caught me in the legs."

"Red" gave him a disgusted look and said, "That was pretty stupid. I can't get you out until morning because you're not in danger of losing life or limb. I know it has to hurt like hell, but you'll just have to sit there and bear it until morning."

I asked the man what happened to the water buffalo, and he said it was killed. In my imagination, I could see this water buffalo, coming in from the field as he had probably done for years, finding these foul-smelling Americans in his path, and charging to try to get home. Normally docile, these large creatures would often become enraged when Americans were around and could be very dangerous. Many were killed by GIs in self-defense, but, oddly enough, I have seen a ten-year-old girl with a bamboo switch turn the head of a huge bull with a mere tap on the snout when he was about to charge me.

Since we weren't able to medevac the wounded man, an idea came to me that I thought might be worth a try. I got up and went out to where the "rabbit" was set up. "How is the 'rabbit'?" I asked the two specialists.

"Well, sir," they said, "it's not working, but that's nothing new as we told you the other day."

"Come with me," I said. On the way back to the bunker I softly sang a little song, "The 'rabbit' is dead, the 'rabbit' is dead, long live the 'rabbit.'"

Back in the bunker, I called headquarters on the radio. "The 'rabbit' is dead," I said.

The operator on the other end said, "Roger, wait one." After a long period of silence, he came back and said, "There will be a replacement there within an hour. Pack up the old one and send it back on the same chopper."

I then sent the two specialists to fetch the dead "rabbit" and told the wounded man he would be headed for the hospital soon. He was more grateful that I can describe as his wounds were starting to throb with terrible pain. Capt. "Red" did not seem overly impressed but ordered a couple of his men to carry the wounded man to the landing pad. When the chopper came in, we were all sitting on the pad with the boxed "rabbit" and the wounded soldier. I used my hand-held strobe light to bring in the chopper. The night was very dark, and it took some time for the pilot to locate us.

When the chopper landed, the crew chief threw off the replacement "rabbit," and we loaded on the old "rabbit" and the wounded soldier. I yelled in the ear of the crew chief with the sound of the chopper blades whirling above our heads, "This man has grenade fragments in both legs. Take him to the hospital."

"Roger," he said. The chopper lifted off, climbing high above our heads before it turned north toward the hospital at Tay Ninh. To my knowledge, the rabbit never proved to be of any use to us or to anyone else except, of course, to that young man who needed to get to the hospital that night.

Helicopters were very vulnerable at night because Charlie was always out moving around at night, and a 51-caliber machine gun could bring one down if it was in the hands of a good gunner. Note that the enemy heavy machine gun was a 51-caliber while ours was a 50-caliber. Some said that the Communists designed this gun with a slightly larger caliber on purpose. It was thought that in times of shortage, they could use our slightly smaller ammo, but we couldn't use theirs. The same explanation was given for why our mortar was 81mm while theirs was 82mm. I, frankly, don't know whether this is true or not or if it's even ballistically possible. I do know, however, that the enemy never showed any signs of being short of ammunition.

One night, when I was out on a night ambush along the river, I watched a chopper, with his running lights flashing fly across our front, traveling high above from south to north. Suddenly I saw green tracer rounds rise up from the dark ground, climbing toward it. The chopper gave evasive action. I don't know if it was hit or not, but it continued on.

I called the incident and the location into headquarters, and, within an hour, a "Puff the Magic Dragon" was above the area, spraying the ground with bullets. "Puff" was a large cargo-type chopper fitted with machine guns that could put a bullet into every square foot of a football field within a few minutes. This "Puff" shot up the area intermittently for about an hour. I don't know whether it hit the VCs who shot at the chopper or not.

Soon after the arrival of the American rifle company, the enemy gave them, and us, a welcoming salvo of mortar rounds. It was late afternoon when it started. Capt. "Red" was in our bunker, cooking a package of freeze-dried shrimp. The mortar rounds began landing in the village and inside our compound with their characteristic sound, a loud but dull thump. We all looked at each other and yelled, "Mortars!"

Capt. "Red" immediately ran outside, which didn't seem like the smart thing to do, and I followed. As I stepped outside, I saw "Red" assembling his 81mm mortar crew. He turned, looked at me, and yelled, "Give me a coordinate, and I'll return fire!"

I ran up to the porch of the headquarters building where our Vietnamese lieutenant was already on his radio, getting the suspected position of the VC mortars. As soon as I got them from the lieutenant, I wrote the coordinates down and called them out to his crew. Then I watched in amazed admiration as "Red" stood there with his crew, shirtless with his hands on his hips, barking out orders as the enemy mortar rounds landed inside our compound. Some were very close, but he never flinched.

After ordering his crew to fire several rounds, he told me to also give the coordinates to his artillery forward observer (FO), who ran over and stood next to me on the porch. The FO was a young first lieutenant artillery officer, who was a little overweight with a slightly pudgy face. He had an olive complexion and dark, curly hair. I will never forget the look on his face. He was terrified. The mortar rounds were also falling near our position on the porch, and there was no cover to get behind. The numerous holes in the roof testified to the fact that the VC had long ago known the coordinates of this building and used it as their favorite target.

The American FO was so nervous that he was shaking all over. He could hardly give the fire mission over his radio. Looking at him made me realize that I had changed. I was still afraid but had somehow become used to the danger. Soon after the firing started, dead and wounded soldiers were brought in and laid out on the floor. I still felt sympathy for them, but the feeling was not as sharp as before. I had also become accustomed to seeing death and injury. After several rounds were fired from Capt "Red's" mortars, including a salvo from the artillery, the incoming enemy rounds abruptly ceased. I suspect that Charlie learned that day that if he was going to shoot at us again while the Americans were there, he had better be ready to clear out fast.

One day Capt. "Red" came by and invited me to go up the river with him to Tay Ninh City in a boat. This sounded like a good adventure, and I agreed. When we arrived at the shore, I was surprised to see a small 16-foot aluminum boat with an outboard motor. I guess I was expecting something larger, such as, a navy PT boat, and I must admit that I was a bit concerned. Nevertheless, I stepped aboard with "Red" and four of his enlisted men. I noticed that his first sergeant was not along, assuming that he, too, thought it was not a very wise mode of travel.

The trip up the Vam Co Dong river was very pleasant. It was a fair day and the wind created by the motion of the boat was cooling. It reminded me of carefree, lazy days as a boy on the York River back home in Virginia. The river was fairly wide and we motored up the middle, which I felt gave us some welcomed distance from possible snipers along the shore. We arrived at the dock at Tay Ninh about midday. There was a large market situated there, which was full of merchandise, produce, and people. The hustle and bustle of the market presented a feeling of normal commerce, which made thoughts of the war seem out of place and far off. I had arranged for our jeep to be waiting, and we all went in separate directions with an understanding that we would meet back at the dock at midday for the return trip back to Ben Cau. I went to province headquarters and to the PX but couldn't buy much because of the limited carrying capacity of the boat.

At the appointed hour, I arrived back at the dock to find the others already waiting. We all knew that it was important to get back well before dark because Charlie basically ruled the dark. Plus anything moving at night was potentially fair game for our aircraft to shoot up. The trip back started out as pleasantly as before, but I felt more uneasy, knowing that anytime you traveled out to somewhere in the morning, the enemy might be waiting for your return that afternoon along the same route. As we motored down the river, we all fixed our eyes on the shoreline with our rifles at the ready. I watched the shore to our right.

After we had been traveling approximately thirty minutes, staying to the middle of the river, I spied movement in the water next to the shore about 200 meters away. After a few seconds of watching the moving object intently, I was able to identify it as a man who appeared to be in the water near the shore with his shoulders and head visible. His right arm was extended straight up, and he appeared to be waving at us. I immediately tapped Capt. "Red" on the shoulder and pointed at the man in the river. "Red" motioned the driver of the boat to head toward him.

As we drew closer to the shore, all sorts of thoughts went though my head. I could tell that he was a young Vietnamese man with medium-length black hair. I wondered if it was a trick, a ploy to get us closer to the shore so that his buddies could fire on us with rifles and rocket launchers. Or was it someone in trouble, perhaps a fisherman or a civilian who was injured and needed help?

As we got closer, I became certain it was trouble and raised my rifle in readiness.

When we got within thirty or forty feet of the man, the situation became clear. The young man was dead. His eyes were open but rolled back in his head. He had apparently died with his right arm outstretched, frozen in an extended position. As the waves from the river lapped against the shore, he swayed back and forth so that he appeared to be waving his arm. As the pilot pulled the boat away to continue down the river, I turned and watched him floating there, waving good-bye as we moved away. He seemed to be staring at us as if he had something he wanted to say from the grave, perhaps something like, "You had better be careful. I didn't think I would end up like this, and it could happen to you."

I assume this man was a dead VC, probably killed in some battle, perhaps in the night ambush we sprung just a few weeks before. He had been left to float aimlessly up and down the river. In my own mind, I dubbed him "the imposter" because he was obviously dead but seemed to be pretending to be alive. There were dead bodies like that scattered all over Vietnam. Sometimes the peasants would bury them, as they had after our ambush, but often they would just leave their dead where they fell, as evidenced by the fact that we occasionally found human skeletons in the jungle while out on patrol. We continued down the river without further incident and arrived back home in Ben Cau safely. When I close my eyes and think about it, I can still see "the imposter's" face.

UH1 helicopter, sporting a picture of "Annie Fannie" on the bow. This Vietnam-era helicopter has been called the "workhorse chopper" of the U.S. Army. It was manned by a pilot, a copilot, a crew chief, and a door gunner with a mounted M60 (30-caliber) machine gun. It could be equipped with rockets to serve as a gunship and could transport six to eight American soldiers or eight to ten Vietnamese. MAT 66 was totally dependant on helicopters for transportation and supply in and out of Ben Cau because of the lack of secure roads.

CHAPTER 17

THE SUPPLY CHOPPER

Swing low, sweet chariot, coming for to carry me home...

—African American Spiritual

It was the day of the army-navy football game in November 1969 when the supply chopper went into the river. Because we were in an insecure area at Ben Cau, we could not drive on the roads and had to leave our jeep at province headquarters in Tay Ninh. We were almost entirely dependent upon helicopters for transportation except for the occasional ride on the back of a Honda motorcycle. The cost was twenty-five cents for a short ride to the next village.

The supply chopper made the rounds every other day to outlying areas such as ours, and a supply sergeant, SFC Wallace, made the trip each time it flew. He was a friendly fellow and we talked some when I took trips into headquarters. One day he confided to me that he was becoming concerned that he might meet with some mishap since he was flying every day and sometimes over unfriendly, unsecured areas.

On the day of the army-navy football game, the helicopter pilot and his copilot had made up some fliers that read "Army beats Navy," and they decided to fly low over the navy dock and throw them out for the navy guys to see. On one of their passes, they flew too low, and one of their skids went into the water, causing the chopper to flip and crash into the river. The crew chief and the door gunner were both killed as they crashed through the windshield. The copilot was declared dead although his body was never recovered. Our supply sergeant, another passenger, and the pilot survived.

A few days later, I took a helicopter from Ben Cau into Tay Ninh. I was the only passenger, and I leaned back, looking out the open door, thinking I would enjoy the short trip and take in the scenery along the way. This pilot chose to fly very low, traveling only about ten feet off the ground in open areas and rising to just above the trees when we came to tree lines. I had heard of this technique, which was used to come up on the enemy suddenly to avoid early detection, but it seemed out of place on a routine flight to headquarters.

Soon we were flying up the river, and we were fast approaching a long, narrow sampan that was loaded down with people and produce and was slowly moving up the river toward the market in Tay Ninh. When we got close to the boat, the pilot dipped his craft down so that the wind from the blades upset the boat, sending people and goods into the water.

I was furious, and with the recent crash of the supply chopper on my mind, I reached up and tapped the door gunner on the shoulder. "Tell that asshole if he does that again, I'll turn him in!" I yelled above the din of the chopper noise.

The door gunner, a large burly specialist grade 4 (spec 4), gave me a hard look and then turned around and once again leaned into his machine gun. I watched to see if he said anything into his intercom mike, which was plugged into the pilot and the copilot. There was no visible movement of his mouth, so I reached up and tapped him on the shoulder again, and yelled, "Tell him!" This time I saw him speak into his mike, and I turned quickly to observe the reaction of the pilot. The pilot and the copilot both turned and looked at me. The thought briefly occurred to me that two of them could jump me and throw me out of the chopper, and no one would ever know what happened to me. I stared back, with as stern a look as I could muster, and adjusted my M16 rifle to remind them I was armed. The pilot immediately looked forward and lifted the chopper up to a respectable height.

The downing of the supply chopper on the day of the army-navy game had shown that such antics were likely to end in disaster, but that was not what made me so upset. What really made me angry was the thought that these yoyos were out there dumping people into the river and doing who knows what else, while we were out in the boonies trying to win the hearts and minds of the people. It further emphasized how difficult our job was becoming. When we arrived at headquarters, I went straight to the office and informed the S1 officer that the work chopper pilot was dumping civilians into the river.

He didn't seem to be too happy to receive the information, but I don't know if anything ever came of it.

A week later, the new supply chopper landed and out jumped Sergeant Wallace with his right arm in a cast. "A bit soon for you to be back on this thing, isn't it?" I asked.

"No, sir," he said. "I'm fine. Besides, it's boring just sitting around camp, so I decided to come back out."

"OK," I said, "but you be careful." He assured me he would and then flashed a smile as he jumped back on the chopper for the trip back to headquarters. I began to worry that his luck really would run out.

As I've said before, I tried to get into Tay Ninh once a week, and a week or so later I found myself on the work chopper with Sergeant Wallace and two American first lieutenants, who were stationed with a mobile advisory team in a remote outpost in the sector north of us called War Zone C. One of the officers was black, the other white, and it was obvious they were good friends and enjoyed working together. The flight to Tay Ninh was short, and we soon found ourselves walking across the runway, comparing notes about what we needed to do and what time we would need to be back at the airstrip for the flight back. It was agreed that we would meet at the NCO Club when we were finished with our work.

I really didn't have much to do except to pick up the mail and a case of beer. I was looking forward mostly to having a relaxing mixed drink back at the NCO Club. These trips to headquarters were like a brief return to civilization, and it was a nice respite from the rugged life back at Ben Cau.

Thirty minutes before our agreed departure time, I went to the NCO Club and sat down at the bar. After considering my choices of mixed drinks, I ordered a tall, cool gin and tonic packed full of ice. As I took my first couple of delightful sips from the drink, I saw the two lieutenants and Sergeant Wallace, his arm still in a cast and sling, come into the bar. They were finished with their business and anxious to get back on the chopper, which they said, was on the airstrip ready to go. I suggested they sit down and join me for a drink, but they would have nothing of it. The supply sergeant told me that another chopper would be leaving in about thirty minutes to deliver a barrel of gasoline to another outpost, and I could wait and catch that one back to Ben Cau. Looking at that cool drink sitting in front of me, I readily agreed.

After finishing the drink, I went out to the airstrip and found the second chopper with a fifty-five-gallon drum of gasoline sitting next to it. I helped the door gunner and the pilot load the gas, which I remember as being very heavy, and we took off for Ben Cau. The flight was short, and upon returning, I walked into our bunker where I found everyone sitting around, listening to our command radio. They all looked up and stared at me as though they had seen a ghost.

"What's going on?" I asked.

Mack spoke up and said in an excited tone of voice, "The supply chopper went down, and we thought you were on it!"

I glanced at Dave, who gave me a quick stare and looked away, saying, "We thought you had gone and gotten yourself killed just when we were getting used to you."

"What about the two lieutenants and the supply sergeant?" I asked.

"It sounds like they're all dead," someone said.

Stunned, I collapsed on my bunk and listened to the conversations going back and forth over the radio net as various people called in reports of the incident. It soon became evident that the VC shot down the chopper, using a 51-caliber machine gun. The chopper crashed and everyone was killed. The supply sergeant's luck had, indeed, run out, and the two happy-go-lucky lieutenants I had talked to just that morning were gone.

I was moved more by this escape than all the other close encounters I had had with mortar rounds, rockets, and rifle bullets. The mood was more somber than usual that evening in the bunker as we went through our normal routine. It went unexpressed, but I know that each man realized that he could have been on that chopper when it went down. I was especially moved and shaken by the thought that I would have certainly been killed if events had been just a little different. I had been saved by a gin and tonic. It was Ironic that the desire for a cold drink actually saved my life, but it seems that life is like that at times and there is no explaining why these things happen. That night, I woke up in the middle of the night and couldn't sleep. When I did get back to sleep, I dreamed I saw Death standing at the foot of my bed in a black hood. I thought again about Dave's words, "Our mothers are praying for us."

Since leaving the war, I have thought a lot about why some men die while others go on living. Why do two men pass through a patch of jungle and one loses a leg to a booby trap while the other goes unharmed? Why does a mortar round come screaming aimlessly down from the sky and kill one man and not another. Is it just a matter of luck, good or bad, or is it Providence? I don't know the answer. For some reason unknown to me, many of us who escaped often feel guilty. All I know is that I was spared, so that today, many years later,

I can sit in the comfort of my home and write this account. I cannot think on it too much, though, because sometimes the guilt is more than I can bear.

I know an older man, Ed Parungo, who is a retired Marine and a veteran of WWII, Korea, and Vietnam. One morning as we talked over a cup of coffee, he told me about a friend of his who had recently died. He said his friend had been severely wounded in Korea and had survived to live a long life but had finally died of complications from his wounds. Ed said, "I escaped without being injured, and sometimes I feel guilty about it."

I just nodded my head and said, "I know."

Sergeant First Class Melvin Davis is sitting in the middle among several Vietnamese soldiers. Our RF company was in a blocking position for a large operation and saw no action that day. Note the Vietnamese officer standing at the table, studying a map of the area.

Left to right: The Vietnamese first sergeant at Thai Thong, Sergeant First Class Mack Rice, Sergeant Liam (our interpreter), Sergeant First Class Melvin Davis, and the team's dog, Smoky.

CHAPTER 18

A VILLAGE NEAR TAY NINH CITY

Wars may be fought with
weapons, but they are won by
men. It is the spirit of the men
who follow and of the man who
leads that gains the victory.

—George S. Patton
Cavalry Journal (September 1933)

Sometime in November, I went to province headquarters and talked with a first lieutenant I had known at Fort Benning, who was now serving on province staff. He told me that he had received an early-out to go back to school and that I should try for one, too. Under the Nixon administration's stated goal of reducing the number of troops in Vietnam, the army was starting to cut back, and he thought I could probably qualify for one.

I had been thinking of going to graduate school when I got back in April, but this would give me an opportunity to start in February if approved. I put in the application, and it was eventually approved. I also put in for R&R, one or two weeks of rest and recuperation, which was given to every soldier after six months of service. My R&R was scheduled for the week just before Christmas.

The early-out was approved to release me sometime in February before the second semester started at the University of Richmond. Knowing that in a little more than a month I would go on R&R and then in a little more than a month after that I would go home made the rest of my tour much more bearable.

Most infantry officers served six months in the field in Vietnam and were then transferred to some sort of staff job for the second half of their tour. Since I was scheduled to get the early-out, I would be required to spend all of my time in the field exposed to combat. I decided it was worth it and determined to stick it out in the field but try not to get killed in the process.

In the middle of November, our team left Ben Cau for good and went to another post at Thai Thong, a small village near Tay Ninh City just a short distance from the 25th Infantry Division base camp. The 25th Infantry was located in a very large fortified post that held a PX and other facilities. There was a small church on the base, and I attended services there at least once. I remember that it was a pretty, little chapel with an open sanctuary that was held up with large, curved, wooden beams. The walls and the beams had numerous holes in them that looked like they had been made by machine gun rounds, probably from enemy 51-caliber guns.

Just before we left Ben Cau, an army chaplain visited us. He was a captain, very amiable, and of course he wanted to talk with us about God and our role as soldiers. We all gathered around and listened intently. It is said that there are no atheists in foxholes, and we were no exception. He said that he knew our situation was difficult, living in this remote place, far from our homes and loved ones but that God loved us and that we should never forget he is with us during our trials.

The chaplain gave us each a small paperback Bible and then hopped back on the chopper to return to wherever he came. I never knew where he was stationed or how he even knew where to find us, but I appreciated his visit and kept the Bible for a long time although I do not know where it is now. He also gave each of us a small plastic cross, which glowed in the dark. I still have that cross, and I keep it on the nightstand next to my bed. It has lost a lot of its glow, but sometimes when I wake up in the middle of the night, I pick it up and look at it, and it gives me a sense of peace.

That night I wrote in a letter to my mother, whom I later discovered had saved all my letters, "The chaplain came to see us today. It is good to hear the Good Word every now and then to remind us there is still hope for the world. Sometimes I wonder if we can ever be forgiven for what we must do to our fellow man."

I can tell by the date on the letter that I wrote those words soon after the battle in Cambodia and that the thought of the eleven VC I had killed was weighing heavily on my conscious. I went on to say in my letter, "It doesn't bother me too much because I know the enemy will do the same thing to me if he gets the chance. I must do it to him first before he can get us, but I know that does not make it morally right."

I think that it was about this time that I decided that there really is a God. This was partly because I had seen the Devil, and I reasoned that if there is a Devil, there must also be a God. I came to realize, and I still believe it today, that Jesus was right when he called the Devil the "Prince of the Earth." I had seen him in Vietnam, and I knew that he was alive and well and living in the hearts of men. He is not choosy with whom he inhabits, and at that time, I found him in all sorts of men, both Vietnamese and American, and at times I even found him lurking in myself. I decided that if there exists such profound evil in the world, there must also be a counterbalancing force for good, and that must be God.

Although Thai Thong was a small village, the setting and the people were more urban than at Ben Cau. We could use our jeep to go back and forth to Tay Ninh City and the 25th Infantry base camp over paved roads. The road through the village, however, was dirt, as usual.

About this time, Nea was replaced with another interpreter named Liam. Like Nea, Liam was a likable young man who spoke excellent English and would accompany us on each operation. He was smaller than Nea and almost boyish in appearance. I was sorry to see Nea go. He was very young and very immature, but I had grown to like him. He had been with us on the ambush out of Go Dau Ha where he performed well. Also he had become extremely proficient with English, and I remember him telling me one day, that he could understand much more that he heard from Americans than he could speak.

As usual, we spent a couple of days unpacking our gear and getting settled. Dave directed the setup of our new home, which was in a large sandbag bunker about the same size as the one at Ben Cau. The roof was lower, however, and I had a problem hitting my head on the beams supporting the roof inside.

The Vietnamese group commander was a captain and the second in command was a young second lieutenant. I liked the lieutenant, who reminded me of the young lieutenant at Ben Cau, but I had a bad feeling about the captain based on information I received from Liam. Among other things, Liam told me that the captain ran a brothel near the gate of the 25th Infantry Division base camp that he called the "Car Wash." Like most Vietnamese structures, it was a modest, wooden building, and it had "Car Wash" painted across the front in large letters. As time went on I would find much more to dislike about this Vietnamese officer.

Our little post was situated next to the small village of Thai Thong, and surrounded by Vietnamese homes. For this reason, our Vietnamese soldiers were reluctant to fire into the perimeter of the fort. One night at about 1300 hours, I was awakened by Liam, who said there was movement in the perimeter. He asked me to come forward. I slipped on my pants and boots and followed Liam to a bunker on one corner of the fort.

The Vietnamese lieutenant, Lt. Lo, was there. He said that his men had seen movement in the wire and he wanted my advice about what he should do. The VC had men we called "sappers," who were especially trained to work their way through the barbed wire while carrying a satchel of explosives. They would move stealthily thorough the wire and booby traps surrounding our forts, wearing almost no clothes in order to avoid snagging on the barbs. When they got close enough, they would light the fuse on the explosive and heave it into the fort. Since they generally had excellent intelligence about our positions, they knew where to throw the satchel to do the most damage, usually at the ammo bunker or the command bunker.

I suggested that the lieutenant fire a few machine-gun rounds into the suspicious area, which was a technique we called "recon by fire." He responded that he was reluctant to do this for fear that he would hit some friendly hut or shop in the area. I understood, but I thought to myself, someday the VC will attack this position in force, and he will have to respond aggressively or be overrun. In the meantime, I realized that he was right.

I turned to Liam and asked him to ask the lieutenant if he had an M79 grenade launcher. When the lieutenant responded yes, I asked him to bring it to me. A soldier appeared quickly with the launcher and a bag full of rounds. I loaded one grenade round and fired it into the suspicious area I had been shown earlier. "Is that OK?" I asked the soldier who had seen the movement.

"Number one, number one," he responded, meaning that I was right on target.

I reloaded and fired again and then handed the launcher to the soldier. "If you see or hear again, you shoot. OK?"

In the dim light of the bunker, I could see him smile, and he said, "OK."

During the night, I heard him lob a few more rounds into the perimeter, but in the morning, daylight showed us no bodies. There was, however, a dark spot on the ground that the lieutenant said was blood. I still thought it might have been sappers and reasoned that the 40mm grenades had either scared them off, or, if we had made contact with the enemy, that they had left with their wounded or dead in tow.

I was always amazed at how some things did not seem naturally to occur to my Vietnamese counterparts. I feared that their enemy, the NVA and the VC, would be more aggressive and more innovative given the chance after we left. I tried to impart what knowledge I could, but I couldn't give them the will to fight, which would make the difference in the end. I would soon learn that this unit suffered from a distinct lack of leadership, making it almost impossible for them to be a really effective fighting force.

Soon after our arrival in Thai Thong, Dave discovered that this company had a Four-duce mortar in the compound that the Vietnamese did not know how to use. It had probably never been fired. The Four-duce was the largest mortar in the infantry's arsenal. It was too large to be carried very far and was usually kept in a permanent compound where it could stay put. Dave got together a mortar crew and taught them how to fire the weapon. I was happy with this bit of initiative on his part and felt that it would improve their chances in case of a future attack.

After only a few days at our new assignment, Liam came to me and said that the Vietnamese group commander was inviting the entire team to a dinner he had planned in our honor. The dinner was held at midday as usual because of the lack of electricity and the danger involved in going out at night. We all assembled in a low, tin-roofed, clapboard building that served as the local restaurant. All of our people attended, which at that time consisted of Dave, Mack, our new medic, Liam, and me. The Vietnamese contingent consisted of the group commander, his two lieutenants, and an assortment of NCOs.

The meal was good by Vietnamese standards. There was plenty of chicken, duck, green vegetables, rice, and loaves of freshly baked French bread. There was also lots of cold 33 beer to wash it down. We all ate and drank our fill, and everyone seemed to enjoy himself.

When the meal was over, the captain stood up to make a speech. He spoke for a short time in Vietnamese, which Liam translated for us. He said that he was very glad that we were there. He said he missed very much the two American lieutenants who had been there before, who had been killed when the VC shot down the helicopter. He went on to say that he knew that we would all be great friends. He closed his speech by saying that he wanted us to provide gasoline, which he would sell, and we would all make a lot of money.

As I listened to him, I was able to put together some pieces of a puzzle that had escaped me before. The two American lieutenants he spoke of were the two young men I had ridden with to Tay Ninh that day the supply chopper went down, killing all aboard. I had missed the return trip because I stayed in the NCO Club to finish my drink. When I did leave Tay Ninh to return to Ben Cau, I rode on a chopper that was delivering a fifty-five-gallon drum of gasoline to this post, apparently to be sold by the Vietnamese captain.

My counterpart was a real operator, an entrepreneur, who had apparently been able to enlist the aid of my deceased predecessors in his scam. He naturally assumed that we would take over their roll, which probably involved participating in the ill-gotten revenue and possibly involving complimentary visits to his whorehouse, the "Car Wash." He was operating more like a two-bit godfather than a military commander.

While he was speaking, I noticed that this captain never mentioned anything about why we were supposed to be there, which was to help him fight the war and help provide security for his region. After mulling all this over for a few seconds, I stood up to reply. Speaking through Liam, I said, "We are very happy to be here, and we thank you for this delicious meal. I also hope that we will all be friends, but there will be no gasoline to sell. We will provide only what we need for our own vehicles. We will help you in any way we can to fight the VC." Then I said in Vietnamese, "*Chung ta giet VC,*" which means, "Together we kill the VC."

The captain, who was still standing, frowned at me and said in English, "Yes, kill the VC, but we need gas."

I answered, "There will be no gasoline." Upon hearing this, the captain turned abruptly and walked out of the room. We all stood up and left in silence. As we left the room, I looked at Dave, wondering if I had done the right thing. He was grinning from ear to ear.

I wasn't sure what I was dealing with or how pervasive the corruption was. The captain seemed to be very open about what he was doing and not concerned about being admonished by his superiors. This led me to think that one or more senior officers at province headquarters may have been involved. I resolved to stay away from him if possible, but I was determined not to be intimidated.

About a week later, I received orders to go on a group-sized operation into War Zone C. I knew this company would be more like a reinforced company as far as size was concerned. A full infantry platoon should number about forty men; however, most units were under strength. A platoon for both Americans and Vietnamese was more likely to have about twenty-five to thirty men. A fully complemented rifle company should comprise around 160 men, but in Vietnam at that time we were more likely to field around sixty to eighty men on an operation that was supposed to be company size.

War Zone C comprised all of the area north and west of Tay Ninh City and was predominantly uninhabited and uncultivated except for a couple of small villages and the land immediately surrounding them. By 1969 a large portion of South Vietnam had been abandoned by the peasants because of insecurity and was no longer producing rice. This had caused the country to move from being a major exporter of rice to becoming a major importer of rice. The American government tried to bring in rice grown in the United States, but the Vietnamese people did not like it, preferring rice grown and imported from other Southeast Asian countries.

We had not been assigned an operation since arriving some two weeks earlier, and I had begun to wonder if they ever went out. Finally, the orders came over the radio one night. The route we had been assigned was fairly short, and I calculated it would probably take only four or five hours to complete. We were transported by helicopter to a large clearing, which was covered with grass about thirty inches tall. I suspected that this field had once been a rice paddy that had been allowed to overgrow.

Much to my surprise, the Vietnamese captain was leading the operation. I had figured him to be the kind of commander who would stay in camp when the troops went out. Besides, I thought he was probably too busy with his enterprises to spend time out in the field. Perhaps the lack of having gasoline to sell gave him extra time on his hands. Or perhaps he felt compelled to show me that he did spend some of his time trying to fight the VC.

The operation started out fairly well. The company fell into a line as we started across the field. The Vietnamese captain, Dave, Liam, and I walked about nine or ten men back from the point man with our radio operators. After crossing the field, we moved into the woods still in a line. As we proceeded down a trail in the trees, I realized this was not typical jungle. The trees were spread apart, and there was sparse underbrush. After awhile, I recognized that the trees were rubber trees and we were walking through an abandoned rubber plantation.

Soon after entering the forest, we came upon a small pond that had been formed by a small dam across the stream. The beauty of this land captured my attention, and I almost forgot we were a combat patrol in the middle of potential enemy territory. As we proceeded down the trail, I suddenly heard a loud explosion behind us. I sensed that the explosion was not normal and involved the spraying of water. Nevertheless, I instinctively dove for the ground as I turned slightly to view the source of the explosion. I immediately realized that one of the men had thrown a hand grenade into the pond in an attempt to kill fish. I sprang back into a standing position and faced the pond. The Vietnamese soldiers broke into laughter as a few small fish floated to the top.

I turned to Liam and said, "Tell the captain that this is very bad, number ten, because if there are VC around, they will know we are here." Liam translated what I said to the captain, who only shrugged and continued up the trail. As we walked through the woods, it occurred to me that we were very vulnerable to ambush. There was basically no point man, and because of the sparse undergrowth, the terrain offered good attack positions from the sides. Also, the ground began to undulate, providing elevated ambush spots where the enemy could pour fire down upon us if they were properly positioned.

I told Liam to tell the captain that we needed to put men out on the flanks and that the point man needed to walk several paces ahead of the rest of the column. The "point" was the most dangerous position on an operation, and it was normal for it to be rotated among the men to spread out the danger. If there were trouble, the point man was most likely to receive the brunt of it, but it was essential to have him out front to avoid leading the whole unit into an ambush. The captain listened to Liam, shrugged again, and continued on without doing what I had suggested.

It became quite apparent that Dai uy was not going to do anything to protect the column. I turned to Liam again, and told him in a firm voice that I insisted that Dai uy take the action I had suggested. This time Dai uy stopped and looked at me. Observing the firm expression on my face, he gave orders for one man to go out to each flank and ordered one of the other men to proceed to point. I felt better and continued to be amazed at the natural beauty of the countryside we were traveling through. Since the going was more difficult for the flank men, it was necessary for the whole column to slow down the pace. After awhile, I realized that the flank men had rejoined the column. We had speeded up but were once again exposed to ambush from the sides.

My patience expired. First there had been the irresponsible throwing of the grenade, and now this pitiful excuse of a commander was trying to lead us all into an ambush with total disregard for the well-being of his troops. He was probably anxious to get back to his cathouse and didn't like being slowed down by something as mundane as good security measures.

My job was to advise, not to provide gasoline, so I decided it was time to advise. At the top of my voice I yelled, "Stop!" It worked even though probably half the men didn't know what "stop" meant. They did stop, and everyone turned to stare at me. I turned to Liam, and, still speaking at the top of my voice, said, "Tell Dai uy this is the most screwed up operation I have ever seen!" Liam's mouth fell open. He was speechless. He was afraid to speak these words to a superior Vietnamese officer. "Tell him!" I yelled. "And tell him exactly the way I said it."

Liam spoke in a barely audible voice, but I do believe he repeated what I had said word for word. At this point, he was probably more afraid of me than he was of the captain. When he had finished speaking, I said in a lower but still firm voice, "And tell him that if he doesn't straighten it out, I will make a report when we get back that he will not like." Liam repeated this with a little more ease than the first time.

The Captain gave me a look that could kill. I had done the unforgivable. I had caused him to lose face. I knew it, but I didn't care because I knew that someday these men would be gravely tested, and they would not only lose face, they would lose their lives. The flank men moved back out to their positions without orders, and we completed the operation in strained silence.

I felt sorry for these units because I knew that someday we would leave and that the VC and their NVA partners would attack and that these men would have no idea how to defend themselves or carry out a mission. The problem was not with the troops but with the leadership. Their commander was both incompetent and corrupt, a deadly combination. I let my boss, Major Petty, know what I thought. Even though the captain was supposed to be my counterpart, I don't believe I ever saw this Vietnamese officer again after this operation.

Fortunately, Lt. Lo, the young Vietnamese second lieutenant in charge of the company that occupied our compound, was more responsible than his superior, the captain. He came to me early during our stay at Thai Thong and asked me what he should be doing. I told him that during the day, he should be sending out patrols into the countryside to keep the VC at bay and to let the people know that his company was in charge. Also, I told him that he should be putting out small ambush patrols at night in order to stop the VC from moving freely into and out of the village. He implemented the suggestions and seemed to be eager to do what he could to improve the situation.

Night ambushes can be one of the most effective weapons against an insurgency. To be effective, an insurgency needs to be able to move about, and generally a lot of this movement will take place under the cover of night. To survive and accomplish its mission, an insurgency needs, at the minimum, three things.

Like all combatant forces, an insurgency needs a steady source of supplies, arms, and ammunition. Secondly, it needs good intelligence, and thirdly, it needs to be able to move about in order to satisfy the first two needs and to be able to conduct operations against the enemy. Particularly in rural areas, the ambush is the ideal way to restrict this movement. It will generally work only in conjunction with a curfew because, otherwise, there is a considerable danger of attacking innocent civilians.

If the insurgency has a considerable amount of sympathy from the local population, it will have the intelligence it needs. In Tay Ninh Province, the local support was probably much larger than any of us imagined. When the enemy is being fed good intelligence, there are two dangers in planning and conducting ambushes that need to be considered. The first obvious problem is that the enemy will be told of the location of the ambush and avoid the area. A greater danger results if the insurgency has enough prior knowledge to actually ambush the ambush patrol as it moves into position. To forestall both of these catastrophes, it is important for the ambush patrol to avoid establishing known patterns. It should never set up in the same place twice in a row, and it should occasionally set up in one location and then move after dark to another location near by. Moving an ambush is dangerous, as we have seen in the nighttime disaster at Ben Cau, but it is sometimes necessary. Two patrols should never be moved at the same time in the same vicinity.

It is noteworthy that the above discussion about the three needs of the insurgency makes it clear that the insurgency can only survive where there is at least a modicum of support from the local population. Later we will discuss how we as occupiers actually encourage this support for the enemy and grow the insurgency by our mere presence in the occupied country.

One night at about 0200 hours, Lt. Lo, the Vietnamese company commander, came into our bunker and woke us up. He was very excited and reported through Liam that his ambush patrol, which he had placed at the edge of the village, was in a fight with the VC. I went immediately to the radio and reported to our headquarters. Then I turned back to the lieutenant and asked, "What will you do?" He gave me the right answer, which was that he would take out a patrol to relieve them. I said that we would go with him and turned to tell Mack to get his gear.

Mack was already getting dressed and said, "I'll go with you." I relied heavily on Mack to assist me in these situations, and he accepted the role without complaint.

I hurriedly got dressed, put on my boots without socks, and grabbed my rifle and satchel of ammo. I went outside to find the lieutenant waiting with about ten men in full battle gear. Mack joined us shortly, and we all went out of the fort through the barbed-wire perimeter. We first completed a short walk down the paved road that ran between Tay Ninh and the 25th Division headquarters.

When we arrived at the intersection with the dirt road that lead to the village, we turned right and headed down a long road that ran through the middle of a large field. As we started down the road, I could hear sporadic firing but not what you would expect from a full-fledged firefight. We quickly covered the distance through the field and entered the north side of the village.

As we walked past the grass-covered huts, I wondered if the people living there knew we were passing by. Did they hear us outside? Were they frightened, or were they VC sympathizers who might want to warn the enemy we were coming? Would they perhaps take a shot at us as we passed? As I've said before, we were very seldom out at night in a village. We made it a policy not to move around at night unless we were on ambush or if it was absolutely necessary. There was a partial moon, and as we moved, I could see the village with its grass-roofed huts among the palm trees. I thought to myself that this is beauti ful, like a travel postcard of a tropical paradise. The night and the moonlight hid the filth and the signs of poverty visible in the daylight. Everything had an eerie but romantic glow.

As we made our way through the village, the firing became less frequent, I suspected that the VC were probably disengaging and falling back into the jungle. We had moved a considerable distance at a very rapid rate. When we reached the middle of the village, Lt. Lo halted to let his men rest while he consulted a map. Lo, Mack, and I all got under a poncho and studied the map, aided by the light of a flashlight. The Vietnamese lieutenant pointed to a spot on the map and said that we were there. Then he pointed to another spot at the eastern edge of the village and said that that was where the ambush patrol was located. By now there was no more firing, and I began to worry that we might run into the fleeing VC or an ambush of their making.

Thieu uy spread his men out, and we all proceeded very cautiously. When we got within hearing distance of the ambush spot, the lieutenant called out to his men. A friendly voice answered, and we all moved in. The squad leader reported, showing us the body of a dead VC, lying face down in the path. The sergeant explained that a small patrol of VC, maybe five to seven men, had come walking down the trail that ran beside the village where he and his squad were set up in an L-shaped pattern. His soldier closest to the trail attempted to fire a claymore mine, but it malfunctioned. Then his man opened up with his rifle, dropping this enemy soldier immediately. The other VC fired back, and his men returned fire. After some exchanges of fire, the remaining VC had withdrawn, probably taking some wounded with them.

The squad leader said that he was very disappointed that the claymore malfunctioned because it would have probably wiped out the entire enemy squad. Claymore mines were awesome weapons but were likely to be assembled and disassembled many times before actually being fired. Over time, this one had apparently become defective.

After Thieu uy gathered up the ambush squad and integrated them with our patrol, we walked back through the village and returned safely to our fort. I was extremely impressed with the actions of this Vietnamese lieutenant. First of all, he had taken the initiative to send out an ambush into an area he apparently knew was frequented by the VC. Secondly, his squad was able to set up in an excellent ambush formation. Thirdly, they must have been awake when the VC came, and, lastly, the lieutenant effectively organized and led the relief patrol. I sensed that this officer was much superior to his group commander (the whorehouse pimp and purveyor of misappropriated gasoline).

Early the next morning, I received word to go into Tay Ninh to pick up a newly-arrived second lieutenant, who would be my second in command. His name was Terrance Liebhardt, and I liked him immediately. He was very young and inexperienced but seemed interested in our work and was willing to learn.

I picked him up from headquarters in our jeep. On the way back, I decided to show him around a bit. As we rode through the village, we came upon the body of the dead VC, which had been left in the middle of the village square. The Vietnamese authorities sometimes did this to see who would claim the body. His body was bloated and had already begun to decompose in the hot sun. I was surprised by the sight and didn't want this new lieutenant to think I had brought him here just to see this grisly display. I explained that our men had killed this enemy soldier the night before and had left him here as a warning to sympathizers and potential VC recruits. He seemed a little startled by the scene and had very little to say as we drove back to our fort.

The next day, a Vietnamese soldier came into our bunker at midmorning to say that an anti-personnel mine had been discovered beside the road leading to the village. Mack and I took the jeep to check it out. The dirt road ran through a large field that had tall grass growing along its sides. After we had traversed about half the distance to the village, we encountered some of our soldiers standing beside the road. We stopped the jeep.

One of the soldiers took us to a spot on the right side of the road and pointed to a large, green, metal object. The object was about the size and shape of a football and was covered with small, square, metal projections that were about one-half inch in diameter. I realized that if this thing had exploded, it would have totally destroyed anything in front of it. Mack exclaimed in an excited voice, "The wires are still connected to this thing! We'd better get out of here!"

We jumped back into the jeep and continued up the road until we came to a Vietnamese lieutenant. He explained that they caught a young boy near the detonation device out in the middle of the field. They were not sure whether he was the perpetrator or just a lookout, but, under interrogation, he admitted that the device had been planted in hopes of killing some Americans. When I heard this, I realized that it was me they hoped to get. I had been down that road the day before with Lieutenant Liebhardt, and they were hoping I would come again. I had a fleeting thought that maybe it was the Vietnamese captain rather than the VC who was trying to kill me since we were now enemies of sorts, but I dismissed the thought. I didn't recognize this mine as being anything I had ever seen in the U.S. Army and assumed it was either Chinese- or Russian-made, making it most likely planted by the VC.

I had heard that certain Americans had cash bounties on their heads. I don't know if this was true in my case or not, but it did seem that I was being specifically targeted. I suspected this would not be the last time it would happen, and I took it as a sign that we must be doing something right.

Christmas in Vietnam. This photograph was taken inside the bunker at Thai Thong, a small village near Tay Ninh City. The timbers supporting the roof were low, and the Americans would occasionally bump their heads. Note the Christmas tree in the upper right-hand corner.

CHAPTER 19

R&R AND CHRISTMAS IN VIETNAM

Glory to God in the highest, and on
earth peace, good will toward men.

—The Holy Bible, Luke 2:14 (KJV)

The first three weeks of December were fairly quiet. There were not many operations, and the ones we conducted were relatively uneventful. The days dragged by. Looking back at my letters to my parents, my thoughts were mainly concerned with looking forward to going on R&R. The day to depart finally came approximately two weeks before Christmas. I went into province headquarters the night before my flight left for Saigon. The first lieutenant who processed my early-out invited me to join him at the Officers Club that night. I didn't even know there was an Officers Club and was surprised to learn that one had been set up in a small trailer in the middle of the compound.

Just before dark, I joined about six other officers who met there to have a few, inexpensive drinks. After about an hour and several drinks mixed with lively conversation, I heard several muffled explosions outside that I recognized as incoming mortar rounds. Suddenly, all the lights were shut off and a loud siren sounded. There was a lot of shuffling in the dark, and I soon realized that I was sitting alone in the trailer not knowing were I should go.

I made my way to the door and down the metal stairs with considerable difficulty because my eyes were not yet adjusted to the dark, and, frankly, because
I had drunk too many gin and tonics. As I made my way across the compound,
I didn't feel in any great danger because the mortar rounds seemed to be falling
at the edge of the compound and were infrequent in number. I saw a little light
coming from under a garage door nearby. I went inside. There was a squad of
heavily armed men inside commanded by an E4-grade sergeant. "What's going
on, Sarge?" I asked.

"We're the reaction force," he responded, then added, "Sir, you'd better stay
here with us." It sounded like a good idea to me. After a few minutes, the all-
clear was sounded and we all went back to our quarters.

Early the next morning, I met an Air America plane on the runway to take
me to Saigon for the flight to Hawaii. It was a small, four-seater, and the pilot
suggested I sit up front, which I did. The ride was quite an experience. The
pilot said that he had a few other stops to make before we turned south for Tan
Son Nhat Airport in Saigon. We first headed north, and I was surprised how
quickly we left the relatively flat land of Tay Ninh Province and entered moun-
tainous terrain to the north. The flight was very bumpy as we were buffeted by
high winds. I began to feel sick to my stomach from the combination of the
rough ride and too many drinks from the night before.

Our first stop was a small outpost on a little knoll between two mountain
ranges. The pilot banked heavily and dropped suddenly as he came in for the
landing, a maneuver obviously meant to discourage any VC on the ground
from taking a shot at us. I was sure I was going to throw up and began looking
for a bag or something to put it in. There was nothing, and I only kept it down
through sheer willpower. We were only on the ground a few minutes and then
back into the air. It was again through great effort that I kept the contents of
my stomach in place as we took off and repeated the same procedure at
another outpost. I was greatly relieved when we finally touched down in
Saigon.

The trip to Hawaii the next day was long but filled with great anticipation.
The feeling of leaving a war-torn, poverty-stricken, third world country and
returning to the United States with its clean streets, green, manicured lawns,
and large, sparkling shopping malls was indescribable. I had not had a real,
American hamburger in eight months, and it tasted wonderful. My wife and I
had a rented room near the water, which had an oblique view of the beach
from the balcony. The weather was pleasant, and we left the sliding doors open
to catch the breeze. The first evening there, someone set off a string of fire-

crackers out on the street, and I hit the floor before I could tell myself it was only firecrackers.

Today, soldiers who are in Afghanistan or Iraq are allowed to come home on leave. At that time, it was unheard of to come home for anything other than a family emergency. The soldier could choose between Hawaii, Japan, Australia, or Malaysia for his R&R. Most married men chose Hawaii because of the ease with which their wives could make the trip. The added bonus for me was to be able to touch foot on a little piece of American soil.

Of course, the one week in civilization flew by quickly, and I soon found myself back on a large plane headed back to Vietnam and the war. As I have mentioned, most infantry officers spent six months in the field, took their one week of R&R, and then returned to take some staff job for the rest of their tour. Because of my early-out, however, I didn't get my R&R until after eight months and was returning to my old job at Mobile Advisory Team 66.

On December 24, 1969, I found myself sitting on a bench in Saigon, waiting for a plane to take me back to Tay Ninh. I tried to get some sleep on the hard, wooden bench, but it was not easy to fall asleep. Sometime near morning the Air America plane arrived, and I headed back to Tay Ninh. A little after sunrise, we landed at the Tay Ninh airstrip. It was Christmas morning when I picked up our jeep that had been left for me at province headquarters.

As I drove back, the sun began to get hot, and I began to think about Christmases back in Virginia. I remembered cool mornings; bleak, winter landscapes; and the excitement that came with decorated Christmas trees and brightly wrapped packages. These thoughts of Christmas made me terribly homesick, and as I drove into our compound, I was almost overcome with sadness thinking about loved ones and home so far away.

Surprisingly, when I cut off the motor to the jeep, I thought I heard Christmas music. It seemed out of place in this hot, pagan land, but it was definitely Christmas music. It was coming from our bunker. There were a large number of Vietnamese gathered around, curiously peering through the open doorway. I gently pushed through the people and made my way inside. The first thing I saw was Lt. Liebhardt, sitting in a folding chair, wearing a crudely fashioned Santa outfit. He had on a large, green army shirt with a pillow stuffed under the midsection, and he wore a white beard fashioned from cotton gauze.

On his head he wore a traditional red Santa cap with white ball on the tip. A long line of children formed outside, and Dave and Mack were leading them in one at a time to sit in the lieutenant's lap to hear him say, "HO, HO, HO!" As each child left the bunker, Liebhardt would give them a small wrapped present of candy.

They were all having a great time, and it warmed my heart to see it. For the first time, I realized that Christmas was not a place, and, if you let it, it could come anywhere you happened to be. To my great surprise, our former interpreter, Bock, was there. He greeted me warmly and handed me a Christmas card. I remembered that he was Catholic and felt bad that I didn't have one to give him in return. It was gratifying to realize that he had chosen our team with which to spend his Christmas. He had Christmas dinner with us and spent the night. I enjoyed catching up with him on his adventures since he had left our team some five months before. Like the Grinch, the Vietnam War had tried to steal Christmas, but it had come anyway, thanks to my great band of men.

The next day Lieutenant Liebhardt came to me and said that he needed to talk with me about something that had happened while I was gone. I suggested that we go outside. Once outside, he told me that the Vietnamese group commander had come to see him a few days after I had left and had invited him to go with him in his jeep.

After riding around a bit, the captain took him to his "Car Wash" (his bar and whorehouse). He was given free drinks, and while distracted, was left there by the captain without transportation. Having consumed a few too many drinks, he was not aware at first of his predicament. Eventually, though, he realized he had been abandoned by the captain and had no transportation to take back to our fort. He had to walk the whole way back, about four kilometers, in the dark, alone—a very risky venture for an American in that part of Vietnam. He went on to say that the next day, the captain came by and demanded that he procure gasoline for him in payment for the entertainment he received the night before at the "Car Wash."

"I hope you didn't give it to him," I said.

"No," he answered, "not yet."

"Not ever," I blurted. "I've told that bastard that there will be no gasoline, and you need to stay away from him. Do you understand? And don't ever do anything like that again."

"Yes, sir," Liebhardt said. I think he was relieved to know that he did not owe the captain anything and readily accepted the admonishment.

Within a week, we received orders to move again, and I knew that someone had wisely determined that my counterpart and I were never going to get along. Before we left, the Vietnamese S3, Major Trang, showed up and presented me with another Cross of Gallantry with Bronze Star. He knew that I would be going home soon and wanted to show his appreciation. I assumed that he, at least, was not part of the gasoline scam.

I'm afraid that this example of corruption with the Vietnamese captain is very prevalent in most third world countries. This man, who was obviously both incompetent and corrupt, had probably received his appointment through a system of favoritism, perhaps because he had a family member in high office.

Sergeant First Class Rice, second from left, and Lieutenant Liebhardt, center, prepare to go on a combat operation with the RF company from Thai Thong. The company commander of this unit was the young Vietnamese lieutenant, second from right. This officer was quite competent, but he was saddled with a group commander who was not only incompetent but also corrupt. When the team would not participate in a scheme to steal gasoline to sell on the black market, the group commander had MAT 66 transferred to a remote village in War Zone C.

Medical clinic held at Thai Thong. Our MAT 66 medic, fourth from right, who was nicknamed "Buddha" by the Vietnamese because of his physical resemblance to the ancient, religious figure, is treating the people of the village. Liam translates, and the Vietnamese company commander records the names of the patients. This was an important effort by advisory teams to help win the hearts and minds of the people.

CHAPTER 20

MO CONG, THE LAST ASSIGNMENT

As for man, his days are like grass;
he flourishes like a flower of the field;
the wind blows over it, and it is gone,
and its place knows it no more.

—The Holy Bible, Psalm 103:15-16(NIV)

The week after Christmas we received orders to move to a village located in the middle of War Zone C called Mo Cong. We were to arrive there by January 10, 1970, and since it was not near the river, we were to haul all of our gear there by truck. I knew that this would be my last move since I was to leave Vietnam by the first of February to start the graduate program at the University of Richmond.

I began to realize how Lieutenant "Short" must have felt. I did not want to be killed or maimed during my last couple of weeks in the "Nam." I decided that once we had made the move, I would guard my movements very closely and try not to expose myself to the VC, who were apparently determined to kill me. Although we were going into a very insecure area, I hoped that our stay there for the next couple of weeks would be uneventful. This was not to be the case.

On the morning of January 10, we packed up all of our equipment and loaded it onto a large military truck. Our new commander, Major Petty, showed up the day of the move to send us off. He said he had been working on getting my Silver Star approved but that my former commander had pigeon-holed it. He said that it now looked like it would be approved and that I should receive it when I returned home. I never did. The real story could not be told, which was that our Vietnamese counterparts had run off, leaving Mack and me alone to evacuate their wounded and bring fire upon the enemy.

The road to Mo Cong was dirt, not paved, and full of holes. Dave and I went ahead in the truck since it would be too dangerous to have the jeep there. The roads were not secure, but it was assumed that we could make one trip without incident before the VC knew what we were doing. I told the others to come in by chopper. The road was really terrible and we were jostled about like beans in a child's rattle.

When we arrived, the rest of the team was waiting, and we unloaded and set up our operation. This bunker was similar to the other ones that we had used. It was located next to the Vietnamese mess hall and the Vietnamese company headquarters. As before, we were located inside a fortified position surrounded by barbed wire, booby traps, and mines. Our fort was located next to the village of Mo Cong, whose major claim to fame was that it contained a large Catholic church. I viewed this as a good sign since Vietnamese Catholics were generally known to be firmly opposed to the Communists.

We were fairly adept at moving by now and the setup went smoothly. By nightfall, everything was in place, and we were ready for our usual pinochle game. That night, I stretched out on my bunk and thought about home. It seemed a long way off in both distance and time, but the thought of it warmed my heart.

The next morning, we were awakened at dawn by the sound of an explosion that sounded like it had come from within the village. I assumed it was a mortar round. In a few minutes, some Vietnamese soldiers came into our compound, carrying an older man who was seriously wounded. Our medic attended to him while I called for a medevac chopper to pick him up and take him to the hospital. The soldiers explained that he had been wounded, not by a mortar round, as we suspected, but by a mine that had been buried in the road and had detonated when he had run over it with his oxcart.

As I put down the mike to the radio, there was another explosion in the direction of the village. Soon a young boy was brought in with serious wounds to his legs. We were told that he had been riding in a truck with his father when they, also, hit a mine in the road. The father had been killed by the blast.

After alerting the chopper that it would have two passengers rather than one, I decided that I needed to check out the situation. Despite the fact that I was "short," duty demanded that I go to the scene of this destruction. Dave volunteered to go with me, and we put on our gear. I carried my shotgun while Dave brought an M16, and we went out of the fort and into the village.

As we traveled down the dirt street, a large number of the people came out of their houses and watched us. They were silent and watched with serious expressions on their faces. I was not sure whether they viewed us as the good guys or the bad guys. Their village had probably been fairly quiet until we arrived. As we passed by, a boy of nine or ten years old called out, "Cowboy!"

I took it as a compliment although it could have been meant as something else. I realized that by then I probably did look like a cowboy. I was tall and lanky with a moustache that was a bit too long for military standards. My shotgun was slung across my right shoulder, and my big knife hung from my left side. I did not feel like a cowboy, though. I felt more like a young man who yearned to return to his home and loved ones. I was only weeks away from leaving and was too "short" to be heading down that dusty road toward a scene of death and destruction.

As we approached the gate to the village, I saw a group of Vietnamese soldiers standing on the other side. I saw a shattered oxcart in the middle of the road with the injured ox kneeling on the ground beside it. A truck with its front cab blown apart sat in a hole to the left side of the road.

The horrible scene told its own story. The oxcart had come down the middle of the road first, loaded with produce, driven by the farmer who was now on his way to the hospital in a U.S. helicopter. The wheel of the cart had hit the first mine, seriously wounding both driver and ox. A few minutes later, the truck had come along, driven by the father with his young son as passenger. Seeing the demolished cart in the road, the driver of the truck decided to pull off the road to the left and go around the cart to avoid any additional mines. The VC had anticipated that someone might choose this strategy and had planted another mine in just the right spot at the side of the road. The left wheel of the truck struck it, wounding the son and killing the father. His lifeless body still lay by the side of the road.

The question was why? Why would the VC want to kill and hurt innocent farmers coming into town for the morning market? The answer was simple. The VC were not after them at all. They were after Dave and me because we had just traveled down the road the evening before. Once again they had assumed, or hoped, that if we had used an unsecured road one day to come in, we would use it the next day to go out. I took it personally. I felt that they were after me. They didn't know or care that I was going home in a couple of weeks.

After Dave, the Vietnamese lieutenant, and I had discussed the situation a bit, we agreed that there were probably more mines planted in or around the stretch of road from the village gate back to where the oxcart lay. Dave called headquarters on our radio and requested that a minesweeping team be sent to clear the road.

While we waited for the minesweeping team, some of the people from the village came and retrieved the body of the truck driver. During this time I asked the Vietnamese lieutenant if we should shoot the ox and put him out of his misery. He gave me an incredulous look and explained that if we did that, the meat would begin to spoil in the hot sun. Hopefully, the ox would stay alive until they could arrange to have him butchered and the meat preserved.

After about an hour, two young American soldiers arrived by helicopter with a minesweeper. I showed them the stretch of suspicious road and told them to get to work. One of them raised his hands in a defensive gesture and said that they didn't know anything about sweeping for mines. They had only been instructed to drop off the minesweeper and bring it back when we were through with it.

I looked at Dave and asked him what we should do. "I can operate the sweeper," he said, "but only if you'll probe. I won't do it with any of these gooks." I knew that "probe" meant that I would be the person to use a knife to probe into the earth when he heard a signal from the detector, indicating that metal was present.

"OK," I said, "let's get it over with."

We started at the gate of the village. As we moved down the road, Dave swept the instrument back and forth across the road in front of us from shoulder to shoulder. I walked behind him. Each time he heard the familiar beep through the earphones, indicating that there was metal below the surface, I knelt down and pushed my big USN MK 2 knife into the earth, looking for the object. Although I had never done this before, I had received instruction on the procedure at Fort Benning. The trick was to slide the knife in at just the right angle so that if it did strike a mine, it would harmlessly strike the metallic side and not the detonator that was on the top.

As we moved along, we found scores of metallic objects, mostly tin cans and rifle shell casings. I was amazed at how many shell casings were found in the middle of a well-traveled road. How many, I wondered, were probably scattered all over the countryside? At lunchtime we stopped to eat a lunch of C rations washed down by Cokes. We bought the Cokes from boys who delivered their beverages from small ice chests attached to the handlebars of their bicycles.

After lunch we continued our tedious procedure until we arrived at a suspicious spot. From the start, we had identified this spot as a likely location for a mine because of the disturbed appearance of the earth. Dave moved the metal detector over the spot and stopped, indicating metal below. I gently pushed the tip of my seven-inch knife blade into the earth at the proper angle. After only a few probes, the tip of the knife hit against a hard object, emitting an audible clink.

I carefully used the knife to scrap away the dirt in front of the object, exposing the smooth, green, curved side of a land mine. Dave took off the earphones and set the detector to the side. He then used his hands to scrape away about six inches of dirt in front of the mine. I stood up and asked the Vietnamese lieutenant if he had any C4 explosive we could use to explode the mine in place. Before he could answer, one of the two specialists who had brought out the sweeper hollered that he had some.

Someone back at headquarters had thought of everything, except, of course, the people to do the sweeping and the probing. The young man produced from his pack a small block of C4 explosive, wire, blasting caps, and a small hand-held detonator. Dave took the blasting cap first, which he crimped onto the end of the wire. Then he pushed the end of the cap into the block of C4, which looked like a small block of white molding clay, and placed it in the hole next to the exposed side of the mine. He uncoiled the wire as we walked back down the edge of the road to a small berm of earth at the side. We knelt down behind the berm, whereupon Dave attached the detonator to the end of the wire and handed it to me. I didn't know why he handed it to me, but I took it in my right hand and squeezed it hard twice.

The resulting explosion was tremendous, causing dirt and other debris to fall on us behind the berm. When I stood up, I saw a hole in the road that was about six feet in diameter and approximately four feet deep. This hole was much larger than the ones left when the truck and the oxcart were destroyed. I figured this was because the force of those mines alone had been directed upward, while the force of the combined C4 and this mine had had been vectored partly downward.

Dave and I continued sweeping down the road until we were satisfied there were no more mines. We then handed the minesweeper back to the two specialists and headed back through the village toward the bunker. "You did a good job with that situation," I said to Dave. He said it was nothing, but I knew that his vast experience had made all the difference.

As we walked back to the bunker, I began to think about our service in the "Nam" over the past nine months. I was mostly satisfied with our performance. We had done our best to provide advice and support to our counterparts, but I realized that perhaps sometimes we had been too quick to do things *for* them, as we had done that morning. I hoped that perhaps now our Vietnamese counterparts, who had observed the minesweeping procedure, would better know what to do in a similar situation when we left. Nevertheless, I continued to worry that they would not measure up.

As for the VC, I knew that they were tough and resourceful. They had targeted our team because we were the enemy invaders, intruders in their land. Perhaps also, they had specifically targeted us because they feared that we were making a difference. We had interrupted their movement up and down the river with our patrols and ambushes. They no longer ruled the night with impunity. I had learned that when you have an insurgency that relies on the cover of night to move about and intimidate the populace, there is nothing quite like a few well-placed ambushes to disrupt their movement.

Additionally, we had dared to attack them in their sanctuary in Cambodia, risking not only injury from their mortars and machine gun fire but also risking political repercussion by crossing the boundary that had protected them. As I thought about our team and its performance over the last nine months, I realized that we had indeed made a difference. I also realized that the VC were probably keenly aware of this success and had most likely specifically targeted our team because of it.

My remaining time at Mo Cong was relatively uneventful. Once again, my Vietnamese counterpart turned out to be less competent than I would have wanted. He was a young first lieutenant, who stayed drunk the entire second week we were there. He also brought in a prostitute who also was drunk most of the time and pranced around the compound in her pajamas when she was not servicing the lieutenant. I asked Liam to try and find out what was going on. He brought in the platoon sergeant, who explained that the lieutenant was on some sort of vacation. I thought it unfortunate that he didn't go to Saigon or some other place to do his vacationing where his antics would not be played out in front of his men. I decided his performance was not that surprising given that his superior was the group commander of "Car Wash" and gasoline sales fame.

The real power in the village, I soon discovered, was the local Catholic priest. He came to visit with us one day, and we went with him to see his church, which was quite an edifice by Vietnamese standards. It was surprising to find this priest and his sizable congregation out in the middle of War Zone C. Lt. Liebhardt, a Catholic, began to spend a lot of time with the priest, and I felt that this was probably not a bad thing, since the priest was such an important part of the village.

The priest had built and equipped a medical clinic next to the church building. One day, Lt. Liebhardt came to me and said, "Trung uy, the priest would like for our medic to come to his clinic and treat the people."

Since this was a function our medic was supposed to perform, I said, "Sure." Then as an afterthought I said, "Of course, we'll need to treat *all* of the villagers, not just his congregation."

As Liebhardt left, I noticed a worried look on his face that told me we might have trouble. Soon he came back and said that the priest did not intend to invite non-Catholics to the clinic. "Then he'll have to do it without our medic," I said.

"But," Liebhardt protested, "the clinic and the medicine belong to him and his church."

"No," I said, "we have to serve all of the people."

Liebhardt was obviously torn between feelings of loyalty to his commander and fidelity to his newfound spiritual leader. Tentatively he said, "But we could only use his medicine."

"No," I said firmly. As he left to give the priest the bad news, I called after him, "Ask the priest what he thinks Jesus would say." The clinic was held a few days later with our medic attending, and all of the people in the village were invited. There was a large turnout, and many sick or injured people were helped.

The day finally came for me to start the journey back to the United States. On the day before my official departure, I took the work chopper into Tay Ninh. Before leaving, I told Mack and Lt. Liebhardt good-bye, and wished them good luck. Dave and Mack were both rotating in March. Liebhardt had just arrived in November, and, of course, had a good deal of time left on his tour. Dave volunteered to go with me to headquarters and drive me to Saigon.

At Tay Ninh, we picked up our jeep and headed south down Highway No. 22. We stopped along the way at Tra Vo so that I could return the shotgun.

Trung uy An graciously received its return and expressed his sorrow to see me leave. I also told Thieu uy Man and our Mama-san good-bye. Mama-san cried as though I were one of her own children. It was a bittersweet good-bye. I was extremely excited about going home, but I had grown genuinely fond of the people at Tra Vo, and it was hard to say good-bye.

When Dave and I arrived at Saigon, we went immediately to MACV head-quarters where I got my orders and signed up for my flight to the States. My plane would not leave until late the next day, so Dave drove me to the BOQ (Bachelors Officers Quarters) where I would spend the night. Dave helped me carry my gear inside and walked me back to the jeep. "Well, Dave," I said, "This is good-bye." I extended my hand.

He shook my hand, but replied, "Oh, no, this isn't good-bye. I'll spend the night with some friends and come back to see you off in the morning."

"Sure," I said, "That's a great idea." I watched as he climbed into the jeep and drove away, knowing he would not be back. Somehow I knew Dave was not a man who liked good-byes, and he would not be back in the morning. He was as fine a man as I have ever known.

The BOQ was full of men who were going home. They were happy and loud, and there were card games going on all over the room. Bottles of booze passed freely from bunk to bunk, and nobody slept that night. Thoughts of home conquered any attempt to sleep.

When the author left Vietnam to return to America, the commercial airliner unexpectedly flew northwest from the airport in Saigon and circled Nui Ba Dinh, Black Lady Mountain, before turning due east to fly home. As the dominant geographical feature in Tay Ninh Province, this mountain seemed to offer a farewell salute to the young lieutenant who would never forget the time he spent with the officers and men of Mobile Advisory Team 66.

CHAPTER 21

LESSONS LEARNED

*What experience and history teach is this—that nations and governments have never learned
anything from history, or acted upon any lessons they might
have drawn from it.*

—G. W. F. Hegel, *Lectures on Philosophy of World History,*
1830

If there is any good that has come out of the Vietnam experience, it is that we have, hopefully, learned some lessons as a people, a nation, and as a military that will benefit us as we come into future conflicts around the world. Most of all, I hope that we've learned to treat our veterans with more dignity than we did during and after the Vietnam War. A more dignified treatment involves the provision of medical and psychological services as well as the provision for a more positive attitude toward our former combatants.

There has been a lot of discussion about Vietnam veterans and their acclimation to civilian life after returning home. Certainly some have not done well, and their misfortune has been broadly publicized in the media. Our local newspaper ran an article about Jessie Jones Jr., a marine who had earned the Silver Star in Vietnam, but who recently died in jail.

A section from the article read, "Jones, who was 54, died in March after he fell 20 feet over a railing in the Wake County jail. A decorated Vietnam veteran,

Jones fell apart after the war and ended up homeless, sleeping on a cardboard box by an automated teller machine in Boston. A cousin in Raleigh put him up in an apartment, but he often ended up drunk on Poole Road, telling war stories." The article goes on to explain that he fell over the second-story railing while being chased by another inmate with whom he had fought earlier.

The story of the crazed Vietnam veteran is a familiar one seen in the press and in movies, but it is, by far, the exception and not the rule. We have learned that all veterans from all wars have experienced some form of adjustment problems when they return to civilian life. It used to be called "shell shock," or "battle fatigue," but today we call it "post-traumatic stress disorder" (PTSD). Whatever you call it, it's the same thing that any soldier who has seen a lot of combat is likely to experience, but most soldiers adjust and go on living normal lives. Like most returning soldiers, I had disturbing dreams when I returned to the States. At first there were several different dreams, short renditions of things I had seen or done. Soon there was only one dream, which was replayed for me night after night, year after year.

In this dream, I would replay an event that never happened but that I always feared would happen. In the dream, it is night, and I am on the berm of our fort at Ben Cau, looking out into the darkness. A horde of VC begins to rush the fort, firing their guns, and screaming as they come. I lift my rifle and shoot them. I know that I'm hitting them, but they do not fall. They come right up to me, charging, shooting, and screaming, and then I wake up. This dream became so frequent that I would say to myself in my sleep, "Here it comes again." The dream stopped about ten years ago.

A few years ago, a pleasant theme appeared in my dreams. I am back in Vietnam and there is no war. It's sunny, and I'm walking around a large lake with a Vietnamese lieutenant, who is telling me about the facilities there. It's a pleasant stroll in the sunlight, and the lake is quite beautiful. That dream stopped a couple of years ago, and today, as far as Vietnam is concerned, I am dream free. While doing research for this book, I learned that there actually is a large lake in the northeast section of Tay Ninh Province. If it was there during the war, I was not aware of it. In addition to the dreams, I had what I can only describe as mild, nervous ticks that would occur unexpectedly on some days and would wake me up at night.

Despite the dreams, the nervous ticks, and occasionally being startled when a truck backfires, I have led a fairly normal life. So far at least, I have not performed any crazed war-inspired acts, not shot up any bars, and not fallen over any second story rails in the county jail. The other Vietnam vets I have known also seem to be living fairly normal, productive lives.

For the most part, the Hollywood portrayal of Vietnam vets as traumatized, war-crazed misfits has perpetuated the lack of respect and honor for these brave warriors. Even now I will occasionally meet someone who, when learning that I served in Vietnam, will say something like, "That's too bad. I hope you weren't too traumatized by it," or "I'm sorry, I hope it wasn't *too* bad." Occasionally I hear a simple, "Thank you," which feels much better. Figuratively speaking, we may have finally learned that it's time to get the Vietnam vets off the "psycho ward" and into the "halls of valor." The first lesson then is that as a nation we must always separate our warriors from the war, and give them the honor and respect they deserve no matter how unpopular the war may become.

In an attempt to get more information for this book and to refresh my memory regarding dates, names, and events, I went to the National Archives in College Park, Maryland. The experience was both a revelation and a disappointment. My disappointment was due to the sorry and incomplete state of the records. I had requested an archivist pull for me the entire set of files for my old outfit, Advisory Team 90, in Tay Ninh Province. These records went back to 1968 and forward to 1972 when the team was disbanded and the records were removed to MACV headquarters in Saigon. I was told by the archivist that the records sat in storage at MACV until right before the fall of Saigon, whereupon they were hastily removed. Some were apparently lost or left behind.

Nevertheless, I did find some interesting documents, some of which served to support lessons I learned during my service. One of the most remarkable discoveries was a copy of my two-page report about the killing of the Vietnamese boy by the U.S. officer riding in a helicopter. The report states that the boy's name was Nguyen Van Diem and that his age was fourteen. It gives the eyewitness reports of the two other people that I interviewed, one being the boy's brother, Nguyen Van No.

The brother tells the story of the grenades and the shooting and states that he fled when the attack started. When he returned to his brother afterward, he found him shot in the head along with numerous shrapnel wounds to his body. The last paragraph says that the unit working in the area was from Fire Base Sedgwick, which would have made it easy to determine the likely perpetrator of this crime. I found this memo in a file labeled "Unsuitability Reports." There was nothing else in the file that would indicate if the officer in question was ever punished in any way. My earnest hope is that he was severely punished for this unspeakable crime.

In the same file, I also found a report written by the deputy district chief, Han Minh Duc, regarding the woman who was struck in the head by the helicopter flying low on the highway in front of the villa at Tra Vo. Her name was Mrs. Nguyen Thi Kieu, and she was born in 1928, making her forty-two at the time of the incident. I stress "incident" and not "accident." Duc states that she was seriously wounded but still alive on August 6, 1969. The other document I found in this regard was an order from the commanding general of II Field Force, stating that all aircraft in the 25th Infantry Division will be numbered on the bottom for easy identification from the ground. The final paragraph states that, "It is hoped that this action will discourage the activities of irresponsible individuals by facilitating the ready identification of any aircraft engaged in careless and reckless operations which tend to endanger the lives and property of Vietnamese civilians."

The second lesson that we, hopefully, have learned is that atrocities committed by our people must not be tolerated. Reports of charges being filed against some of our soldiers who are accused of committing atrocities in Iraq may mean that we have learned this lesson. Tolerating atrocities is not only morally wrong, it is also bad for the business of winning the hearts and minds of the people we are supposed to be helping.

Another lesson involves certain attitudes of occupied peoples that inevitably develop when a conflict drags on for years without resolution. A particularly interesting memo that I found in Senior Province Advisor Appling's general correspondence file profoundly demonstrates this lesson.

The memo was dated January 27, 1970, and entitled MEMORANDUM OF CONVERSATION. This memo actually records minutes of a meeting that took place between four prominent leaders in Tay Ninh Province. The leaders were Luong Huy, a rich Chinese businessman; Vuong Tinh Dan, finance chief of Nihan Xa Party; Doung Minh Nghia, a wealthy businessman; Trinh Quoc, the high school principal and second deputy secretary-general of the Cao Dai Secular Life Commission; and Michael M. Skol, second secretary of the U.S. Embassy. I assume that Skol was the author of the memo since he was the only American shown as a participant at the meeting. The meeting was held at Nghia's house in Tay Ninh City. The "Subject" of the memo was "Ambivalence."

This memo is so poignant and illustrative of the Vietnamese mindset at that time in their history, that I feel compelled to discuss it point by point.

The first paragraph reads as follows:

1. <u>The American Presence</u>. Luong Huy noted, and the others readily agreed, that most Vietnamese are quite unclear about the prospects of U.S. troop reductions. People appreciated the U.S. contributions and feared the consequences of withdrawal; yet they also disliked the Americans and desperately wanted them to leave Viet-Nam. Nghia flatly stated that "the great majority of Vietnamese hate the Americans only slightly less than they hate the Communists." He assured me that this majority did not include the people in the room.

I submit that the people in the room most likely shared the majority opinion. The difference was that these men knew that if the Americans left and the Communists took over, these leaders would be targeted for execution or internment. As we now know, many Vietnamese leaders such as these fled for their lives on planes for America as the Communists marched across their country in 1975. Many of those who did not leave were interned in "reeducation camps," some for as long as six to eight years.

The second paragraph reads as follows:

2. The four men became particularly agitated while discussing what they considered one of the most significant problems in Vietnamese-American relations: the conduct of U.S. convoys. Recalling specific experiences, they insisted that that conduct was continuously and contemptuously despicable and that "whatever the Americans are trying to do in the development field is being neutralized by the way the trucks—even the military police—run wild round the countryside."

When I read this, I was reminded of a passage from Larry Heinemann's book *Black Virgin Mountain*. This is the same Black Virgin Mountain (Nui Ba Dinh) that I described as sitting roughly in the middle of Tay Ninh Province. Describing his conduct as a young armored personal carrier (APC) driver in 1968, Heinemann confesses, "We generally rode roughshod over the countryside around Cu Chi and Dau Tieng, the Iron Triangle and the Ho Bo and Bo Loi Woods, Tay Ninh City and the Black Virgin Mountain, and I have no doubt we radicalized more southern Vietnamese to Ho Chi Minh's nationalist revolution than we 'saved.'"

The third paragraph of the memo reads as follows:

3. "<u>The Righteous Cause</u>." I suggested that this love/hate of Americans was related to the Vietnamese concept of the "righteous cause" ("chinh nghia"). Trinh Quoc agreed and went on by asserting a paradox which I have heard on several occasions in various forms; "I detest the Communist and could not tolerate their control, yet I believe that they, and not the Government, have the righteous cause." He explained the seeming contradiction: "For as long as I or anyone in my family can remember, the only cause worth supporting was ridding Viet-Nam of foreigners—any foreigners. This is the righteous cause and the Communists are the ones who have never varied in their espousal of it. But the Government has inherited the opposite of this cause: The preservation of foreign influence. I hate the Communist, but they are partly right. I dislike the Government, but prefer it to the other side. I despise the American presence, but I hope they won't leave too fast."

It must have been terribly confusing for these men to have to live with this contradiction and have to face this dilemma. As Americans, we should be able to readily relate to this concept of the "righteous cause." Do we not think of our own American Revolution in terms of a "righteous cause" where we celebrate George Washington's crossing of the Delaware to defeat a superior invading force on Christmas Eve? As a boy I well remember going to Yorktown where I heard a very articulate park ranger tell of how our ragtag army of citizen soldiers whipped the British and drove them from our sacred soil. Do we not also celebrate and applaud the underdog in our literature and movies? The cry of the Alamo still stirs our blood, and our favorite stories, from *The Last of the Mohicans* to *Star Wars*, feature outnumbered, but valiant, heroes, prevailing against larger and better equipped enemies.

The fourth paragraph of this document exposes a regional bias that I, frankly, did not know existed:

4. "<u>We are all Southerners</u>." Speaking, it seemed, for the group, Nghia asserted that another significant aspect of the estrangement between GVN and the people was the geographic composition of the Thieu apparatus. He pointed out that the four men, one Chinese and three Vietnamese, represented various groups in the province, but insisted that they were all nevertheless Southerners. "Most of the people are Southerners, but most of the Government is not Southern. How can we be sure, then, of our leaders?"

Michael Skol concludes his memo with the following:

> 5. Comment: To Vietnamese, at least, the issue of who is the enemy and who is in the right and who genuinely represents whom is not so brightly clear. At any rate, the statistics and ratios and charts tell not half the story.

The "story" has indeed been muddled for many of us for a long time. Tay Ninh may have been different than the rest of Vietnam, but I doubt it. I suspect that the attitudes displayed in this memo were representative of the attitudes in the entire country of South Vietnam.

Sitting in the research room at the National Archives, reading this memo, which had been residing there in a crumpled file for the past thirty-five years, I began to understand a situation I could only dimly see in 1969 when I was a young first lieutenant, living and serving with the Vietnamese people of Tay Ninh Province. I knew then that something was wrong. The people I was advising were not up to the task of defending themselves when we left. Conversely, their opponents were determined, resourceful, dedicated, relentless, ruthless, and willing to suffer great hardship because they had the "righteous cause."

The third lesson, so dramatically presented by this memo, is that when we occupy another country, the longer we stay as an occupying force in that country, the more the occupied people will grow to resent our presence. If there is a resistance force (an insurgency), our mere presence will serve to increase the numbers of the resistance, and over time the resistance will tend to obtain, and our forces will tend to lose, the "righteous cause" in the eyes of the occupied people. Likewise, if we are supporting a local government in the occupied country, that government will also lose the support of the local people if the occupation is allowed to drag on for an extended period of time.

The fourth lesson, which also relates to protracted conflicts, is that if our military becomes bogged down in hostile action that drags on for an extended time without clear goals and a well-defined mission, the result can be serious undermining of the morale of the U.S. military. This situation is also guaranteed to cause the loss of confidence on the part of the American people, especially if casualties continue to be significant.

The fifth lesson, which was so painfully apparent to those American soldiers who operated in areas of Vietnam next to the Cambodian border, is that we must never again give sanctuary to our enemies. Our military must always be able to pursue the enemy and disable, capture, or destroy him wherever he goes. To do anything less violates one of the basic principles that allow an army to be victorious. If an enemy is important enough to fight, expending our country's blood and resources, he should also be important enough to risk the political consequences of taking the fight to wherever he may chose to go.

The sixth lesson that comes to us from the Vietnam experience, involves how we should support our allies who may be involved in a military conflict. If we come into the fight on the side of an ally, particularly if the ally is fighting against an insurgency, we must teach that ally's military to fight in such a way, and with methods, that they can maintain after we leave. A major mistake we made in Vietnam, and I must admit that I was part of it, is that we taught our allies to fight utilizing our massive firepower, artillery and airpower. It's true that when we left Vietnam, we also left our equipment behind, but that equipment rapidly deteriorated without the proper maintenance. By 1975, for instance, a large number of the South Vietnamese helicopters were either immobile or unsafe.

Now that we have all of this information from the failed effort in Vietnam, what value is it? The answer, of course, is that it should be of value to us as we prosecute conflicts in which we are currently involved, Afghanistan and Iraq being most pressing. Additionally, these lessons should be paramount in the minds of our leaders as they may contemplate undertaking any new military adventures.

As for Afghanistan and Iraq, each present different challenges. In the summer of 2006, the situation in Afghanistan seemed to be relatively under control. If however we are not able to continue to reduce our involvement there, and it drags on for years, we may begin to see new challenges. The Taliban, the former regime that we expelled, are now conducting operations against the Afghan government from their bases in Pakistan. We must be careful to observe the principle of denying the enemy sanctuary as we join with our Afghan allies to counter this threat.

To better understand the situation in Iraq, I contacted my old friend and classmate from the University of Richmond, Major General Warren C. Edwards (U.S. Army ret.). When I told Warren that I was trying to relate lessons learned form Vietnam to Iraq, he explained that the situation in Iraq is very complicated and not much like Vietnam. His response was as follows:

> Comparing Iraq to Vietnam is fraught with difficulties. While the continuing conflict in Iraq is generally described as an insurgency, describing it that way is significantly misleading and I believe, has led to significant

errors at the strategic and operational levels. If the insurgency against coalition forces were the only or even the primary problem, it would have been defeated months ago or, at worst, could be allowed to limp along at a relatively low level for many years with little or no US involvement. The problem in Iraq is political and has no direct military solution- either by large numbers of coalition forces or by any type of an advisory effort to train Iraqis. Iraq like much of Africa was cobbled together by the former colonial powers with no regard to ethnic or religious affiliations. Iraqis have no experience with collaborative, representative democracy and have always been united by either a monarch with supreme authority or by a dictatorial regime. Iraq is divided along ethnic lines in the north (Kurd vs. Arab) and religious lines in the south (Sunni vs. Shia). These sectarian divisions dominate and complicate all endeavors. Any political settlement that would allow the sectarian divisions to be submerged even for a time would deal a death blow to the "insurgency" quickly with or without the assistance of the US. The intractable problem is sectarian divisions and not anti-US insurgents.

On the subject of using U.S. advisors to build up the government forces in Iraq, Warren Edwards sent me an article written by Andrew F. Krepinevich, the executive director of the Center for Strategic and Budgetary Assessments and author of *The Army and Vietnam*. This op-ed piece, which is entitled "Send In The Advisers," was published by the *New York Times* on July 11, 2006.

The gist of Krepinevich's argument is that it is very important for advisors to be used extensively to prepare the Iraqi forces to take over as American forces are withdrawn. Calling advisors, "the steel rods around which the newly poured concrete of the Iraq military will harden," he laments that there are presently only 4,000 American advisors in Iraq and says that the number needs to be doubled or tripled. He also remarks that the best officers tend to avoid serving as advisors, saying, "The reason is simple: the Army is far more likely to promote officers who have served with American units than those who are familiar with a foreign military."

When I asked Edwards if he agreed with Krepinevich he responded:

> I agree that advisors can assist Iraqi units to become better trained and more self-sufficient. I have little visibility into the current quality of the advisory effort. What Andy Krepinevich asserts in his article is credible—the tension between regular units and special operations however defined is not new. Krepinevich has a habit of being right. The real question is whether the U.S. strategy for Iraq is a coherent, realistic one. I'm not convinced that simply training ever more Iraqi units with suspect loyalties will

result in success. I have yet to see a policy that deals with an incipient civil war.

The challenge then is for our government to help the Iraqi people to achieve a political solution that in Edward's words can "allow the sectarian divisions to be submerged." Only then can we determine how pervasive and strong is the true insurgency. This political solution will require that the central government in Baghdad be extremely strong and supported by a strong and loyal military, which I believe can best be accomplished with a strong U.S. advisory effort.

Despite these political, sectarian, and regional considerations, I believe that there are still very important lessons from the Vietnam experience that apply to Iraq. If the conflict continues for an extended period of time, accompanied by significant American casualties and a poorly defined mission, there will be a deleterious effect upon the morale of our military, and the American people will continue to express diminishing support. Further, a more protracted stay in Iraq is likely to create more instances of reported atrocities and missteps on the part of our troops, infuriating and radicalizing the local population. The longer we stay the more we will grow whatever real indigenous insurgency exists in the country. Finally, as we move forward with an extensive training program for the Iraqi military, whether through a strong advisory effort or by other means, it will be very important to teach the Iraqis to fight in a way that they can sustain and using equipment that they will have when we leave.

The importance of this last point was dramatically demonstrated to me in 2005 when after a major offensive by U.S. troops on the outskirts of Baghdad, an American colonel was asked in a radio interview why Iraqi forces were not more involved in the attack. He answered that "they are not quite ready yet and they do not have helicopters." I submit that the insurgents also do not have helicopters and that they have probably received considerably less training than our allies.

In the end, the real test will be whether these Iraqi troops, trained or untrained, will pledge their loyalty to the central government or to their particular sectarian, religious groups. The other factor, which is largely beyond the power of our military to influence, is the willingness of the American people to stay the course. If the U.S. does anything other than just abandon the effort, it will probably be necessary to maintain some American presence in Iraq for a long time to come. This will involve the provision of an American military force in Iraq of probably 30,000 to 40,000 soldiers to serve as a deterrent to adventurism from neighboring regimes such as Syria and Iran. Americans were willing to tolerate this level of troop employment in Korea for a long time. Whether they will tolerate it in Iraq is as yet unknown.

A final warning comes to us at least partially from the Vietnam experience. Our U.S. leaders need to be very careful about the roles they expect our military to fulfill, and not be overly ambitious about what they can actually accomplish. In this regard the label "war on terrorism" may be an unfortunate choice of words because it implies that the fight against terrorists here and around the world is something that our military can and should wage. There is actually very little that our military can do except for where a foreign government is obviously and openly supporting terrorists who are attacking us, such as was the situation in Afghanistan. Additionally there may be isolated individual missions against terrorists that our soldiers can undertake, but for the most part the global struggle against terrorism must be waged by other elements of our government such as the CIA, the FBI, Homeland Security, local police forces, and our border and ports authorities. In the meantime our military must stand by until called to do what it does best, which is to destroy our enemies upon the field of battle.

EPILOGUE

When I left Vietnam, I became quickly immersed in my new civilian life and started a rigorous graduate course in business at the University of Richmond. I thought often about the men I had left behind in MAT 66 and Advisory Team 90 but heard very little from them.

In May 1970, I received a letter from Lt. Terrance Liebhardt, saying that he was in the hospital in Cu Chi, suffering from injuries he received when he "ran our jeep off the road and hit a man on a bicycle." He went on to say that the man lived and he, Liebhardt, had a broken leg. The old jeeps did not have the stable, wide configuration of today's Humvees and were fairly easy to overturn. Sadly, he also reported that Maj. Barton had died when his helicopter crashed in Cambodia. I was very sorry to hear this since I had always admired Maj. Barton for his excellence as our S3 officer. I sent a letter back to Terrance but never heard from him again. In fact, I never heard from any of the other men from my team until 2005.

On a second trip to the National Archives, I found other less remarkable but still interesting documents, including:

- an order naming the MACV Advisory Team 90 compound in memory of SSG Gilbert E. Wallace. He was the supply sergeant who was killed when the supply chopper was shot down.

- various after-action reports, regarding the river ambush near Go Dau Ha and the Cambodian incursion;

- a letter from the Vietnamese province chief to the commander of First Brigade, 25th Infantry Division, thanking him for sending Capt. "Red's" company to Ben Cau;

- a casualty report for Lt. Liebhardt, sending him to the U.S. hospital in Cu Chi;

- daily journals that described the crash and retrieval of the helicopter in which Maj. Barton and Maj. Trang were killed, along with a letter from the province senior advisor, Mr. Hugh G. Appling, recommending medals for the helicopter pilots and crews who risked their lives to pick up our wounded in Cambodia. It was gratifying to see that particular letter since I know firsthand that these helicopters returned to their base with numerous shrapnel holes caused by the great number of mortar rounds fired at us on that mission.

I found another document in the National Archives that was the most interesting of all. It was a copy of the documentation awarding the Bronze Star for Valor to SFC Mack F. Rice. I was delighted to find it sitting there with its official citation and my eyewitness report attached. I had always assumed that his recommendation had been lost along with mine when Maj. Barton died in Cambodia. Mack was a fine soldier who always did his duty, and I was gratified to learn that he had received this most deserved award. Armed with this documentation, I was determined to try to locate him when I returned to my home in Raleigh.

I contacted a search company that advertised, "Find your lost military buddies," and gave them what information I had. I knew his full name, his approximate age, and his last known home of record, New York City. A very helpful young lady did the search with me standing by on the telephone and said that she thought she had found him in Hampton, Virginia about forty miles from where I grew up in West Point.

I called the number from my office and listened to a very pleasant woman's voice on the answering machine say that I had reached the Rice residence and to please leave a message. I left a message that I was trying to locate SFC Mack Rice, with whom I had served in Vietnam, and if this was his number would he please call me back. I must say that I was a little nervous when I left the message. After all, it had been thirty-five years. What could have happened to him during all those years? Would he really care to talk to me now after so long? But then I thought about Mack and that easy, friendly way he had, and I decided he probably hadn't changed that much.

About midafternoon that day, the phone rang and I answered it. A rather tentative voice said, "Is there a John Loving there? A Lieutenant John Loving?"

"Mack!" I exclaimed. "Is that really you, Sergeant First Class Mack Rice of Mobile Advisory Team 66 in Tay Ninh, Vietnam?"

There was a soft chuckle on the other end of the line. "Yes, it is. Only I retired a few years ago as a command sergeant major."

"No kidding," I said. "I wondered if you made sergeant major."

"*Command* sergeant major!" he corrected with a chuckle. This is the highest rank that can be achieved by an enlisted man in the U.S. Army and quite an accomplishment for a young, black man from rural South Carolina.

"Mack, I don't know if you realized it, but I thought you were my best man, and I always took you when I expected trouble."

"Well, I did realize that you always took me when there was trouble," he said.

About midway thorough the conversation Mack said, "I was just telling someone about you the other day."

"No kidding. Why?" I asked.

"Well, I was telling them the story about that day the VC chased us out of Cambodia, the day when Dai uy handed you that smoke grenade and took off running."

We had a good laugh about that day although it certainly wasn't funny when it happened. Time seems to mellow both men and events, and we had a good and pleasant talk about those days that we spent together in the "Nam." Before we hung up, I told Mack that I would be coming his way before long to visit my son David in Virginia Beach, and I would stop by to see him.

A few weeks later, I was in the area and Mack and I arranged to meet at a restaurant in downtown Hampton at the waterfront. When he pulled up in front of the restaurant in his white Lincoln, I recognized him immediately, for he had changed remarkably little for a man sixty-five years old. It was a warm, sunny, spring day, and sitting outside on the veranda at the restaurant, we had a wonderful visit. All of the formality that existed between officers and enlisted men in the active army completely faded away.

We both remarked that we had not seen anyone else that we served with in Vietnam in all these years, which was remarkable, considering that Mack was a career man. The visit was warm and friendly, and I enjoyed it immensely. He took me over to Fort Monroe, which was where he spent the last years of his service, helping to run the National ROTC program. We rode around the post, which was very picturesque and packed with history, and he explained each landmark we passed.

It is impossible to explain the bond that can develop between men who have experienced combat together. While you're going through it, you have to be tough, shrug off the danger, and try not to get too close to anyone because they may be taken from you at any moment. You must control your emotions because you must never seem weak, particularly if you're in a leadership role. But years later, sometimes those emotions that have been contained for years can come to the surface, and it can be a very emotional experience.

On Memorial Day, a group of us from the local Veterans of Foreign Wars post went to a local nursing home to meet with the residents and to honor the veterans who are patients there. We had a little ceremony around the flagpole, and after it was over, an older black man in a wheelchair rolled over to me and asked, "Did you say that you have a man here who was in Korea?"

"Yes," I said, "Ed Parungo was in Korea. Would you like to see him?"

"Yes, I was in Korea," he responded. When I brought Ed to him, he looked up with tears in his eyes, and with a broken voice, he said, "I just need to talk with somebody who was there, somebody who understands." He and Ed talked for awhile about things that only they could talk about. It was, essentially, the same for Mack and me.

Back in the parking lot of the restaurant overlooking Chesapeake Bay, Mack and I said good-bye. We were two old warriors with gray hair, but we still had our memories. We shook hands, but it didn't seem to be enough, so very awkwardly we hugged like brothers who had not seen each other for a long time. That hug expressed both the spoken and unspoken words. It was both an honor and a privilege to serve with such a man.

GLOSSARY

AK-47	Standard communist 7.62mm assault rifle carried by VC and NVA soldiers
APC	Armored Personnel Carrier
Article 15	Nonjudicial punishment usually for offenses not serious enough to warrant a court-martial
C4	White, claylike plastic explosives
Charlie	American slang for Vietcong
CIB	Combat Infantry Badge
Claymore	U.S. antipersonnel mine that fires 700 steel balls in a sixty-degree arc
Cobra Gunship	U.S. AHIG attack helicopter
Dai uy	Vietnamese word for "captain"
Dust-off	Medical evacuation by helicopter
81mm Mortar	Indirect fire weapon assigned to U.S. company-level units
82mm Mortar	Standard Communist mortar
FAC	Forward Air Controller
Frag	Fragmentation grenade
Gook	Derisive term for Vietnamese people used by some GIs
GVN	Government of Vietnam

Hooch	Small Vietnamese home
Huey	UH-1 series helicopter
KIA	Killed in Action
LAW	66mm Light Antitank Weapon (disposable, one-shot, shoulder-fired rocket launcher)
LRRP	Long Range Reconnaissance Patrol. A unit of ten to twelve soldiers whose mission was to go out into the countryside and observe enemy movements without being detected, if possible.
LZ	Landing Zone
MACV	Military Assistance Command Vietnam
M16	Standard U.S. 5.56mm semiautomatic/automatic rifle
M60	Standard U.S. 7.62mm machine gun
M79	Standard U.S. 40mm grenade launcher, single shot
Medevac	Medical evacuation by helicopter
MIA	Missing in Action
NCO	Noncommissioned Officer, Sergeant
NVA	North Vietnamese Army
OCS	Officer Candidate School
PF	Popular Forces (small South Vietnamese unit responsible for defending a village)
PX	Post Exchange
RF	Regional Forces (South Vietnamese company-size units responsible for regional security)
R&R	Rest and Recuperation (seven-day, out-of-country leave for U.S military)
ROTC	Reserve Officers Training Course
RPG	Russian-made Rocket Propelled Grenade
S1	Staff personnel officer
S2	Staff intelligence officer

S3	Staff operations officer
Sapper	An enemy soldier trained in infiltration and demolition
Short	Term used to indicate that an American soldier had only a short amount of time remaining on his tour in Vietnam
Thieu uy	Vietnamese word for "second lieutenant"
Trung uy	Vietnamese word for "first lieutenant"
VC	Vietcong (Vietnamese Communist)
WIA	Wounded in Action
XO	Executive officer

SELECTED BIBLIOGRAPHY

Books

Dockery, Martin. *Lost In Translation: A Combat Advisors Story*. New York: Random House, 2003.

Heinemann, Larry. *Black Virgin Mountain: A Return to Vietnam*. New York: Doubleday, 2005.

Lind, Michael. *Vietnam, the Necessary War: A Reinterpretation of America's Most Disastrous Military Conflict*. New York: Touchstone, 2002.

Maclear, Michael. *Vietnam: A Chronicle of the War*. Photography edited by Hal Buell. New York: Black Dog & Leventhal Publishers, Inc., 2003.

Maraniss, David. *They Marched into Sunlight*. New York: Simon & Schuster, 2003.

McDonough, James R. *Platoon Leader: A Memoir of Command in Combat*. New York: Ballantine Books, 1985.

Moore, Lt. Gen. Harold G. (ret.) and Galloway, Joseph L. *We Were Soldiers Once...And Young*. New York: Ballantine Books, 2004.

Tonsetic, Robert. *Warriors: An Infantryman's Memoir of Vietnam*. New York: Ballantine Books, 2004.

Documents

All of the following documents may be viewed at The National Archives, College Park, Md.

Award of the Bronze Star Medal with "V" Device. Rice, Mack F., SFC USA. 12 January 1970.

Dailey Staff Journal of HQ, II Field Force, U.S. Army, South Vietnam, G2 Section, 2 Sep. 1969.

Dailey Staff Journals of HQ, II Field Force, U.S. Army, South Vietnam, G2/G3 Sections, 26 Oct. 1969.

Investigation of the Death of Nguyen Van Dien, memorandum for LTC Cloud by John C. Loving (1LT Inf.), dated 19 Sep. 1969, Tay Ninh Province, South Vietnam.

Letter from Hugh G. Appling, Province Senior Advisor, Tay Ninh Province, South Vietnam, to presiding Judge of Court of Appeals/Tay Ninh, 6 Aug. 1969, Subject: the accident occurred on the highway 22 at Tra-Vo hamlet.

Memorandum of Conversation Re: Ambivalence, Michael M. Skol, Second Secretary of Embassy, Tay Ninh City, South Vietnam, 27 Jan. 1970.

Memorandum from Han Minh Duc, District Chief/Hieu-Thien, to presiding Judge of Court of Appeals/Tay Ninh, dated 6 Aug. 1969, Subject: The accident occurred on the highway 22 at TraVo hamlet.

978-0-595-39107-3
0-595-39107-9

Printed in the United States
202625BV00004B/1-114/A

9 780595 391073